TROPICAL AQUARIUMS

Tropical Aquariums

by Neil Wainwright

With 12 plates in colour by
ERNEST C. MANSELL
*and 12 pages of black and white
photographs*

Line drawings in the text by
BAZ EAST

FREDERICK WARNE & CO LTD
FREDERICK WARNE & CO INC
London   New York

© Frederick Warne & Co Ltd
London, England
1970
Reprinted 1972
Reprinted 1974

Library of Congress Catalog
Card No 72-114793

ISBN 0 7232 1263 5
Printed in Great Britain by
Cox & Wyman Ltd, London, Reading and Fakenham
651.973

Contents

PUBLISHER'S NOTE

The metric measurements given in this book are approximate.

List of Plates

I

The Essential Equipment

WHEN first becoming interested in keeping tropical fish, most beginners make the mistake of having too much equipment. Some will be fortunate enough to be given the various items but even so too much equipment is a mistake, because it encourages the belief that tropical fish-keeping is an expensive hobby.

In this chapter we will first consider the equipment that *must* be owned, and then describe those items that are useful but not absolutely essential.

First, of course, must come the tank itself.

Before deciding on the size and type of tank, its finished appearance must be imagined. When set up and illuminated it will form an eye-catching feature in any room and it must be decided where it should stand to give the most pleasing effect.

To prevent long, trailing leads, the tank must be reasonably close to an electric power point, and to avoid the rapid growth of algae (described in a later chapter) it must not be too close to a window that is exposed to strong sunlight; this will mean, more particularly, one that faces south.

Apart from these two factors there is not a great deal to consider, though the reflection of a lighted tank on a television screen may be a matter of importance to some people!

Next, is it to be a simple tank or a more elaborate piece of furniture?

For the beginner the choice must always be a plain, rectangular tank. Such an item is cheaper than bow-fronted and similar shapings, and if a set-back is experienced a rectangular tank is easy to restore whereas a more imposing variety can be quite troublesome.

The all-glass, one-piece tank sometimes used for goldfish is not suitable for tropical fish. The latter need a tank in which the bottom is of slate or wired glass, with sides of thick glass set in an angle-iron framework. The glass will be held with special aquarium cement.

Tanks may be bought in different sizes but anything too big should be avoided by the beginner. Only one tank should be set up and for this a base size of 21 in. by 12 in. (62 cm by 31 cm) is suggested as being large enough.

Something should be mentioned about tank depth, although if cold-water fish have been kept previously, the following facts will not be new to the prospective keeper of tropicals.

Fish need oxygen to maintain life. In an aquarium the underwater plants produce oxygen, but the amount produced depends on the number and species of plants, some being slightly better 'oxygenators' than others.

The plants cannot possibly produce all the oxygen needed and most of it is drawn from the air in contact with the surface of the water. So, the larger the surface area of the tank the more oxygen there will be for the benefit of the fish in it.

This leads to an important point.

Imagine two tanks of exactly the same surface area, but that tank 'A' is 6 in. (15·25 cm) deep and tank 'B' 2 ft (62 cm) deep. Because of the volume of water it might be thought that tank 'B' could hold four times the number of fish as tank 'A'. Actually, it will only absorb as much oxygen from the air as the smaller tank and with four times the number of fish to share that oxygen they would be in great discomfort.

'Rules' are sometimes suggested to show how many fish can be kept in a tank of particular size, these being worked out at so many 'inches of fish' (less the length of the tail) to so many gallons of water. These rules can lead to serious mistakes unless the depth of the tank is also considered. Reasonable depth is necessary, so that the fish are comfortable and displayed to advantage, but it is water area that is the important factor.

The number of fish in the tank will be considered later. At present it is only necessary to suggest that the beginner's tank should be 12 in. (30 cm to 31 cm) deep.

A tank cover is usually supplied with the tank and this is fitted with a hole to take an electric lamp-holder. (Fluorescent lighting should not be used with aquarium tanks, though some forms of strip lighting are satisfactory.) The inside of the cover should be painted or rust-proofed because there will be considerable condensation.

Electric heaters are made up of an element set in a glass tube (rather like a test tube) and the best type is 'thermostatically controlled'. In other words, it is set (usually at 72°F or 22°C) so that the

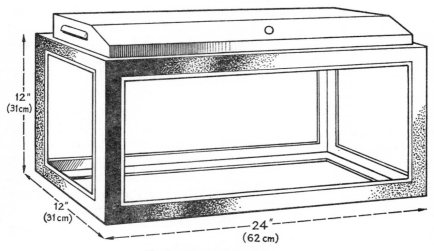

Tank with cover for light

heater switches itself off when the water is being held steady at that temperature and automatically switches on again if the water temperature drops a couple of degrees.

Many beginners, perhaps, get a little concerned about water temperature. Ideally the water should be at a constant heat. But tropical fish are hardier than is usually believed and as those who have lived in the tropics know, temperatures there can sometimes drop sharply at night. Water temperatures will not fall as much as ground temperatures but even so there can be a distinct difference between the day and night conditions, and the fish stand up to this without trouble. A drop of a couple of degrees in the tank is not vital and provided that the water does not become too cold (as might happen during a long power cut) no great harm will be done.

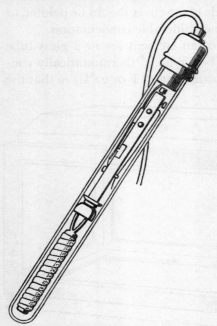

If the water is of the correct heat before the fish are put into the tank, one heater will usually be sufficient to maintain the tank at the proper temperature. Heaters are graded according to the number of watts of electricity they produce, and as a guide it is usually calculated that 8 to 10 watts are needed for every gallon of water. More simply, the larger the tank the larger the capacity of the heater must be, but for really big tanks two smaller capacity heaters (one at each end of the tank) is to be preferred to one large heater.

Heaters are inexpensive and some fish-keepers make

Combined heater/thermostat

certain that a spare is always available in case the one in the tank suffers damage. This is an excellent safety precaution though the buying of a second heater can be postponed until the tank is set up and functioning properly.

A thermometer for testing water temperature is essential. It is possible to buy a type that floats in the tank, but many people feel that these look out of place. With care, water plants can be trained to cover electric leads and so on, but it is difficult to hide a floating thermometer. It is no great hardship to check the temperature every day, using an ordinary small thermometer.

Aquarium gravel is sold for rooting underwater plants. The

4

PLATE 1 · (*Natural size*)

1 & 2. Neon tetra.   3. Belgian flag tetra.   4. Beacon fish.
5. Rosy tetra.   6. Flame fish.

PLATE 2

An example of a
well set up tank.

(photo : Genyk Products
Ltd., Mitcham)

PLATE 3

Angel fish.

PLATE 4 · (*Natural size*)

1. Spotted danio. 2. Zebra fish. 3 & 4. Harlequin fish. 5. Pearl danio.

amount needed must depend on the size of the base of the tank and the depth to which it will be covered, but more will be said about this later. An equal mixture of coarse and fine grade gravel is preferable as this will help to prevent small pockets in the gravel. Such pockets (or 'voids') form traps into which uneaten food can fall, rot, and gradually poison the water, for the

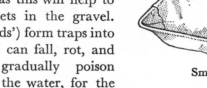

Small net

voids are usually difficult to clean out success-fully. (Neither builders' sand nor garden gravel can be used for the tank. These are quite unsuitable, and may cause harm to the fish.)

Narrow strips of thin lead are of help in anchoring underwater plants during early stages of growth, and planting will be made easier by using a long stick of small end-section, out of the end of which a V-shaped notch has been cut.

Occasionally it will be necessary to catch a fish in the tank and transfer it elsewhere. A small net is necessary and most suppliers stock rectangular nets that are handier in use than the normal round net. Fish are wily and often have to be netted in a corner, and a round net offers too much space round the edges by which they can make a dash for freedom.

Particles of food that fall to the bottom of the tank and rot cause trouble to the fish and affect the colour of the water.

This can be prevented by using a glass siphon tube to suck up the waste. A piece of hollow glass tubing is satisfactory, but it needs to be longer than the depth of the tank and of a

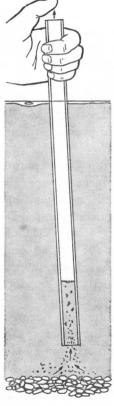

Glass siphon tube

bore large enough to suck up rubbish without getting blocked, yet not so large that it will disturb the plants, etc.

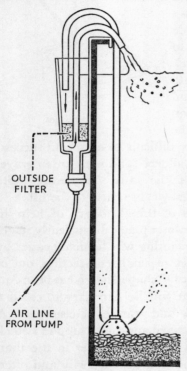

OUTSIDE FILTER

AIR LINE FROM PUMP

Aerator/filter unit

Sometimes it is necessary to clean the inside of the tank glass. For this purpose some fish-keepers use fine steel wool held in the fingers but it is possible to make a simple tool for doing the job.

It consists of a long wooden handle at the end of which is clipped an ordinary razor blade. All cleaning and similar operations must be carried out with as little disturbance as possible, and this is more easily done with the slender tool inside the tank rather than the human hand, which, to the tiny fish, must appear enormous and frightening.

Apart from fish and plants (which are the subjects of separate chapters) the really necessary equipment has now been mentioned. The most expensive item is the tank and such things as the net and scraper could well be home-made.

The first non-essential item that might be mentioned is the aerator, or aquarium pump.

This is a device to pump a continuous stream of bubbles through the tank. The water is gradually circulated so that the water at the bottom of the tank is brought to the top where it absorbs some oxygen from the air. At the same time the water gives up some of its carbon dioxide. The air bubbles themselves release minute quantities of oxygen into the water.

Aerators are of various sizes and are operated electrically. By installing one, more fish can be kept in a given volume of water than with an unaerated tank, but the equipment must be kept going for a reasonable number of hours each day, otherwise the fish population will again have to be reduced.

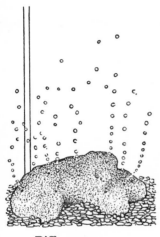

Diffuser stone   Feeding ring

'Diffuser stones' are sometimes used with aerators. These are real or artificial stones drilled so that there are a number of holes on each surface through which air can bubble out. Diffuser 'stems' are similar but are in pipe form.

A filter is sometimes run in conjunction with the aerator and this helps to keep the tank reasonably free from solid matter. It may operate from inside or outside the tank. One of the most popular forms of such equipment is the undergravel or biological filter. With this device a gridwork of perforated tubes is laid in the aquarium gravel. Water is sucked into the tubes by an air-lift, the movement of the water causing a certain amount of aeration. Organic matter in the water is passed down into the gravel, and bacteria living on the individual stones of the compost feed on the organic matter, converting it into plant-fertilising salts and harmless gases; the latter are

7

carried away by the air-lift. In this way the tank is kept clear of sediment.

A 'feeding ring' is a plastic ring into which dried foods are sprinkled as it floats on the water surface. When the food eventually sinks it will be in a restricted area instead of being dispersed and can be more easily cleaned away.

Another device is for feeding white or micro-worms. It is a small

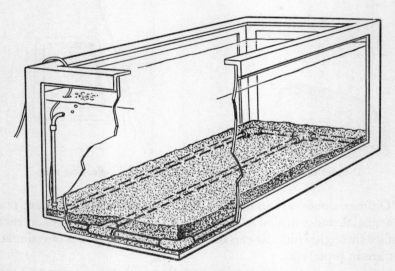

Undergravel or biological filter

plastic container, open at the top, with a suction cap so that it can be fitted inside the tank. The container base has a series of minute holes so that the worms can escape into the tank. By putting the worms into the container they are still available as food, but any soil, etc., will remain in the container, thus helping to keep the tank clean.

The glass siphon tube has already been mentioned. For partially emptying a tank a length of $\frac{1}{2}$ in. ($1 \cdot 2$ cm) diameter rubber hose is useful. With one end of this in the tank, air can be sucked out of the tube until water starts to flow, and it will continue to flow as long as the free end of the hose is lower than the end that is in the tank.

For those who do not like the job of chopping up earthworms for live feeding, a 'shredder' is available. It consists of two stainless steel plates that grind the worm so that it is fed in the form of a pulp.

RUBBER HOSE
TO BUCKET

Siphoning out the debris

Micro-worm
feeder

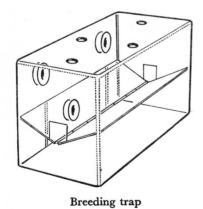

Breeding trap

Various breeding traps are on the market, for use in breeding tanks. One type consists of a small container held inside a larger tank by rubber suckers. This small tank is arranged so that when the mother-to-be is put into it she cannot escape into the main tank. Slots are cut in the bottom of the small container, these being wide enough to allow the fry to swim through, but too narrow for the mother to follow them.

Another trap consists of a series of plastic rods that make a temporary bottom to the tank, the fry escaping through the gaps between the rods and remaining safe beneath them.

Also on sale are a wide range of artificial plants, fancy rockwork and other forms of decoration, but it is obvious that these are not essential for the successful running of a tropical fish tank.

2

Aquatic Plants

HAVING obtained the equipment, the next step will be setting up the tank.

The aquatic plants will be an important feature in the layout, so they should be considered at this point.

It has already been mentioned that the underwater plants help to maintain the oxygen content of the water. Some plants are better oxygenators than others but the differences are not so great that it can be said that any particular species *must* be planted in a tank.

The plants also provide shade (for which the fish will be grateful on occasion) and a safe hiding place for very young fish ('fry'). They also assist in keeping the tank balanced by disposing of certain gases, making use of fish excreta, and so on.

There are two main classes of aquatic plants, described as 'floating' and 'submerged'. In an aquarium the beauty of floating plants may be almost completely hidden so they are only occasionally planted. The submerged plants may never grow to the height of the water in the tank or may reach the top of the water and then trail their leaves over the surface.

It is with the submerged plants that we are chiefly concerned in this chapter.

The plants have been described below in alphabetical order but it is suggested that having noted the details of one or two that appear to be of interest, the beginner should study specimens growing under normal conditions. This is usually possible by visiting a large water-life retail store.

In some ways the plants need as much care in selection as the fish, for they can be responsible for introducing harmful bacteria and organisms into the tank.

Half-grown, healthy-looking plants with abundant leaves are the best to buy. They should not be handled roughly and the seller should lift them by the roots, not the stems, for the latter are often brittle.

The plants must not be allowed to dry out before being set in their tank. They may be brought from the shop wrapped in damp newspaper or hessian, and immediately before planting they may be washed gently under warm running water. Broken or discoloured leaves must be pulled off and it is a sound idea to disinfect the plants in a weak solution of permanganate of potash.

Plants differ in their behaviour after transplanting. Some die back and then recover strongly while others suffer no check at all. In the next chapter it is recommended that the tank be left undisturbed for seven to ten days after planting. If this is done the plants should be in a perfectly healthy condition before the tank is in full use.

Plants need little attention apart from the removal of dead leaves, but one point must be watched. If lead sinkers are used to anchor the plants the stems may be damaged during growth if the lead is too tight. With well-rooted plants it may be possible to remove the collar at a later stage, and where feasible this should be done.

There are some plants which certain people seem unable to grow. It is not a question of water or tank conditions but that the fish-keeper does not have 'green fingers' where that particular species is concerned.

If this happens, and the plant is one which the fish-keeper particularly wants to grow, the following idea can be tried. A small pot is half-filled with a mixture of gravel, loam and a little peat, and the plant put in this. The container can be sunk into the gravel, which is heaped over the pot to hide it. Even the most difficult of plants usually grow well in an enriched soil.

Many underwater plants spread by means of 'runners' that root at a short distance from the parent and start new plants. When the latter are well rooted they can be broken from the parent plant and, if required, they can be replanted elsewhere.

Other plants come from seeds or 'rhizomes'. A rhizome may be thought of as a thick stem growing in the gravel, and if it is cut into thick slices each can grow into a separate plant. Cuttings from an ordinary stem will root well in some cases, and such cuttings will develop into vigorous, healthy plants.

Notes now follow on some of the better-known aquatic plants, but it may be mentioned that some water-life shops make a speciality of dispatching plants by post, and often offer attractive bundles of mixed varieties.

Plants sometimes have alternative names but the most popular name has been given below, so that the seller should be able to recognise what is wanted.

Ambulia is occasionally put on sale under its alternative botanical name of *Limnophila*. It is a submerged oxygenator of handsome appearance, producing small white flowers but sometimes demanding a rather richer aquarium compost than do most of the underwater species. The colour is most unusual, being of rich, almost emerald, green. The leaves are deeply indented and fernlike, the plants tending to mass in dense clumps. Some of the larger fish may pull at the plants as they browse among them, and being tender stemmed the tops may be broken off. The species spreads quickly by means of cuttings and may root from broken pieces resulting from the activities of the fish. *Ambulia* has two species, *Ambulia heterophylla* and *Ambulia sessiliflora*, but the difference between them is relatively unimportant and as far as the tropical fish-keeper is concerned they may be regarded as one plant.

Amazon sword plant is seen at its best in a really large tank when kept well away from other plants. The leaves are light green in colour.

The Amazon sword should never be put in a newly set up tank and it will not thrive in hard water. Once properly established in a tank with rich gravel it grows rapidly, putting up new leaves at intervals of a few days. The leaves are broad, up to 1 in. (2·5 cm) wide, and sword-shaped. The plant is of compact growth habit and spreads by means of runners from the crown.

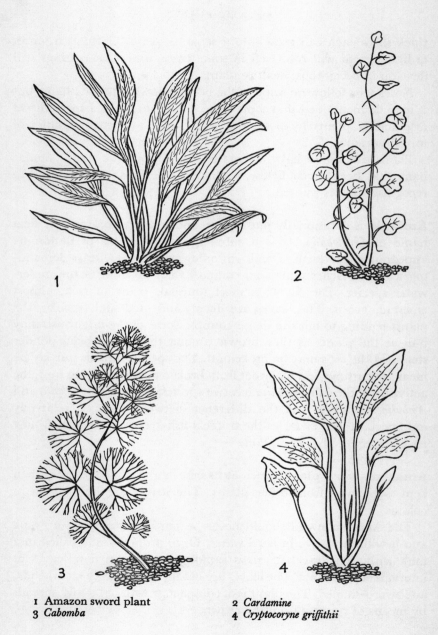

1 Amazon sword plant
3 *Cabomba*
2 *Cardamine*
4 *Cryptocoryne griffithii*

This is considered to be a difficult plant to grow successfully but it is worth while taking trouble with it as it is more attractive than the average underwater plant. A smaller species of the same family, which may be easier to grow, is called the 'chain sword plant'.

Aponogeton   The best variety is of a pea-green colour, with long pointed leaves having wavy edges. The plant is grown from corms in the spring but it needs a high percentage of sand in the gravel; the

Aponogeton

plant dies back in the winter. *Aponogeton* is usually grown in small clumps, though fully grown specimens can be set out singly if preferred. There are various species of *Aponogeton*, some growing to a large size.

Cabomba, with two main species, is an excellent oxygenator that is often sold as fanwort. It grows strongly, soon making its way to the top of the tank, and it is one of the easiest of the aquatics to propagate, a piece pulled from the top of the stem quickly rooting if it is pushed into the aquarium gravel. The plant needs strong lighting if it is to flourish and under such conditions will flower well though the white or yellow flowers are not conspicuous. It is a plant particularly favoured by browsing fish. The stem is brittle with the leaves deeply indented and, like *Ambulia*, almost fernlike.

Cabomba caroliniana has leaves of a deep shade of green, but to add variety to the tank many owners prefer to plant *Cabomba caroliniana* var. *rosaefolia*, which has leaves in a most attractive shade of red.

Cardamine   This is a plant that grows very rapidly during the spring and summer but dies back in the autumn and winter. It can be rooted from cuttings. *Cardamine* is particularly notable for its delicate appearance and pale green colouring. It should be set out in clumps.

Indian or **water fern** (*Ceratopteris thalictroides*)   This is a submerged plant that prefers plenty of bright light and rather shallower water than most aquatics, though it will do well in a tank of average depth. The plant is rather less hardy than the average. It has tiny, pale green leaves that are extremely decorative, the plant sometimes being said to resemble an underwater parsley. To this particular variety the name of water sprite has sometimes been given.

Indian or water fern

There is also a less familiar species (*Ceratopteris pterdoides*) which may be called the floating fern, though it is not a floating plant in the generally understood meaning of the word. The leaves are broader than those of its botanical relative, of a lighter, almost pea-green colour, and the plant may be even more handsome than the normal Indian fern.

Both species produce small ferns on the fronds and stem, these later breaking free to establish themselves as separate plants.

Cryptocoryne   This is a large family of plants and one in which there is some confusion as regards names. For example, one particular species is known to many aquarists as *Cryptocoryne willisii* but is known to others as *Cryptocoryne undulata*.

All the varieties are decorative and are usually planted singly.

They are hardy, but slow in growth compared with many aquatics. A height of 6 in. to 8 in. (15 cm to 20 cm) when fully grown is about standard. Leaves are wavy-edged, bright green or a slightly darker green in colour, though some of the more handsome varieties have leaves in which the underparts are reddish.

All the different species of *Cryptocoryne* are suitable even for comparatively small tanks. In the past *Cryptocoryne willisii* and *Cryptocoryne griffithii* have seemed to be the most favoured species with fish-keepers.

Elodea   This species is frequently sold under its newer title of *Egeria*. It is one of the most prolific of the underwater plants and if not kept under control it will take over the tank and kill the less virile species. Small cuttings root easily; the leaves are bright green.

This is another plant that looks its best when in small clumps. It is unusual in that it seems to grow as well in cold water as in warm, and in fact it will not tolerate water temperatures much in excess of 70°F (21°C). *Elodea*, therefore, cannot be used successfully in breeding tanks.

The species most commonly sold for the aquarium tank is *Elodea densa*.

Hornwort   This is unusual because, although it remains submerged, it does not form an extensive root system. The leaves are bristly. Hornwort is an attractive plant that is at home even in the small tank. The new plants are developed at the ends of the stems in the form of winter buds that sink to the bottom of the tank.

Ludwigia

Ludwigia is a plant having vari-coloured leaves, the upper sides being green and the undersides red or purple. The leaves are large and arranged in pairs, one on either side of the stem. *Ludwigia* is considered to be one of the most

17

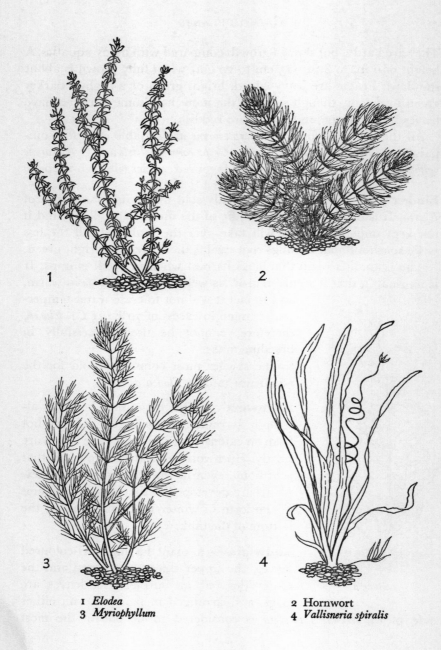

1 *Elodea*
3 *Myriophyllum*

2 Hornwort
4 *Vallisneria spiralis*

decorative of the underwater plants but some experts describe it as a poor oxygen-producer. The plant is hardy and always grows towards the light.

Myriophyllum   This is a particularly useful plant as it is regarded as one of the best oxygenators. It is of very rapid growth habit, and undemanding as regards aquarium gravel, but it must have plenty of light.

Myriophyllum (of which there are several varieties) is a delicate, feathery-looking plant which must be set out in clumps to give the right effect. It roots easily from cuttings taken from the new shoots that come out of the main stem. The chief defect of the plant (which is also known as 'water milfoil') is a tendency to become spindly when the growth is past its best.

Riccia   This liverwort is one of the few floating plants that is of use to the fish-keeper and it is at its best in the breeding tank, as the thalli intertwine and gradually form a matted cover towards the top of the tank. It therefore forms an excellent hiding place for fry, which can remain hidden without being seen from beneath.

The thalli are slender and forked at the ends, and the plant develops a root system. It is claimed that this plant is one of the best natural oxygenators.

Sagittaria   There are several species in this particular genus but probably the most popular among fish-keepers is *Sagittaria natans*. This is another of the grass-like species suitable for planting in clumps.

The leaves may grow to over 1 ft. (30·5 cm) in length and during the summer months small white flowers may be developed above the water. *Sagittaria* is at its best in a community tank that is well established.

In general appearance the plant resembles *Vallisneria* but the leaves are of a darker shade of green. The plant spreads itself by runners.

Salvinia   A floating plant, with round leaves covered with short hairs. It is particularly well suited for the breeding tank as the leaves

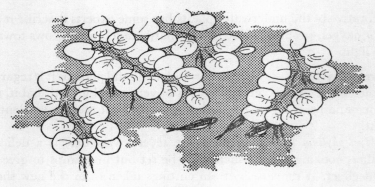

Salvinia

intertwine and form perfect hiding places for the fry. The plants grow rapidly during the spring and summer months, and provided that decayed or yellowed leaves are pulled off, it will remain in good condition for a long time.

Vallisneria   This is one of the most popular of all underwater plants and it is represented in nearly all tanks. There are several varieties of the plant, ranging up to a giant species only suitable for large sized aquaria in zoological gardens, etc. The plants are grass-like, lightish green in colour, and look their best when planted in small clumps.

Vallisneria reproduces itself by means of runners and when well established the new plants should be cut free and transplanted, but being very prolific these plants are likely to get out of hand and overcrowd the tank. When planting, the root crown must not be covered with gravel.

A favourite variety is *Vallisneria spiralis* though this needs a tank certainly not less than 12 in. (30·5 cm) deep. In shallow water the leaves tend to form a twisted mat on the surface, and if this is allowed to spread unchecked the amount of light reaching the water is likely to be seriously curtailed.

Various names (such as 'eel grass' and 'tape grass') have been given to *Vallisneria spiralis,* on account of its twisted stem.

PLATE 5 · (⅔ *natural size*)

1. Rosy barb, male (breeding season).   2. Nigger barb, male (breeding season).   3. Two-spot barb, male (breeding season).   4. Clown barb.

(*photo: L. E. Perkins*)

PLATE 6
Brown acaras.

(*photos: L. E. Perkins*)

(*above*)
Blue gourami.

PLATE 7

(*right*)
Bumble bee.

PLATE 8 · (*Natural size*)

1. Three-striped pencil fish.   2. X-ray fish.   3. Bloodfin.
4. One-striped pencil fish.   5. Feather-fin.

Vallisneria torta (sometimes called 'corkscrew *Vallisneria*') does not grow as high as *spiralis*. The leaves of this species are of a darker shade of green and also somewhat broader than those of *spiralis*. The leaves of *torta* plants are markedly twisted.

3

Setting Up the Aquarium Tank

THE keeper of tropical fish and the angler have to share one particular virtue – which is patience.

Having bought the equipment and made plans for buying the aquatic plants, it might be thought that setting up the tank would be only a matter of a couple of hours' work. Yet, if this part of the job is hurried too much the result will never be really satisfactory.

The first step is to clean the tank thoroughly (both inside and out) with a strong solution of soda, followed with ordinary clean water. At this time the chance should be taken of noting any leaks that may have resulted from the glass being pushed slightly out of place when the tank was moved from shop to home. A slight smear of aquarium cement should cure the leak, and this material can be bought from all water-life stores. This repair work must be done carefully so that only a very little of the cement is exposed to the water in the tank.

The clean tank is then transferred to the table, or wherever it is to stand, remembering that when filled with water it is going to be exceedingly heavy, so the table needs to be a stout one.

Fine and coarse grades of aquarium gravel are mixed together in equal quantities and spread over the bottom of the tank. Ordinary sand or gravel must *not* be used for this purpose.

The gravel need not be spread too evenly as a few slight crests and hollows along the bed will add to the effect. It must also slope from back to front of the tank, being about $1\frac{1}{2}$ in. (3·75 cm) high at the back and $\frac{1}{2}$ in. (1·2 cm) at the front. Once the water has been put in the tank this slope will not be so noticeable but if the gravel is spread to a uniform depth the water will make it appear that it is heaped up towards the front.

With the gravel laid, the tank has to be filled with water, and a few words about this will not be out of place.

Water that is absolutely chemically pure is not suitable either for plant or fish life, but on the other hand there are wide variations in the acid or alkaline content of water in different areas.

When more advanced books and magazines about the hobby are read it will be found that a great deal is written about the 'pH' of water. The beginner should not worry about this and, at this stage, the meaning of pH will not be explained. A little knowledge can be dangerous, and any attempt to 'improve' the local water supply often has unfortunate results.

Fish can adapt themselves to a considerable variation in water content and all that the fish-keeper really needs to know is whether the local water supply is hard or soft. The former type of water is, of course, responsible for the 'furring' that develops in water pipes, kettles, and so on.

Water should never be put into the tank direct from the tap and it must be allowed to stand in an open container for some hours before it is used. This will rid it of the chlorine smell that is noticeable with some town water supplies.

If the local water is soft, no further action need be taken but if hard it should be boiled and the top half only of the water should be put into the fish tank. In spite of what is commonly believed, filtered rain water is not essential for tropical fish tanks.

To pour the water direct on to the gravel will disturb it to such an extent that the work of laying will have been wasted.

There are two ways in which the water can be put into the tank without disturbing the gravel. The latter can be covered with a sheet of newspaper or (preferably) thin polythene, and the water poured gently on to this. Alternatively, a cup can be stood in the bottom of the tank and the water poured into this very gently until it overflows the edges and runs down on to the gravel. The newspaper or polythene sheet will float up and can be removed when there is about 3 in. (7·5 cm) of water in the tank. The cup may be taken away when the water level in the tank is level with its rim.

The water should be poured into the tank until it is about half full, then the heater and aquatic plants should be put into place.

The heater must not be buried in the gravel. Some forms of heater have a suction pad by means of which they can be fastened to the glass, but if such a pad is not provided the heater must be laid on the gravel and more or less anchored there (either by plants or a small piece of rock-work) but in such a way that most of the heater is in contact with the water.

It is always something of a problem to get the heater into a good position without its being too noticeable, but with care it can be done.

Some fish-keepers like to see some natural stone-work in the bottom of the tank. The only objection to this is that if the stone is not of good shape it can provide small pockets into which uneaten food will fall and rot. On the other hand, if it is properly arranged the rock-work can form useful hiding places for the smaller fish when they find life getting too exciting. The stone-work must be carefully arranged so that it cannot fall, and there must not be too much of it. The stones should be put in boiling water to sterilise them before they are put into the tank.

There is some argument between fish-keepers as to whether aquarium ornaments should be used. If there are not too many they can look quite effective, but when aiming at realism Chinese pagodas and fairy castles are not wanted. Should such ornaments be used they should be put in place when the tank is half full.

In setting out the underwater plants the rule must be small plants to the front of the tank and large at the back, but the species concerned must also be considered. Some plants (for example, *Vallisneria*) look best when set out in small clumps, while others can be left in isolation. It must always be remembered that plants tend to spread quickly and accordingly the tank should not be over-planted.

As there are no fish in the tank there is no objection to the hands being plunged into it, though in an occupied tank a forked stick or something similar should be used in planting, so as to disturb the fish as little as possible. Plant roots should be spread well out into the gravel, and to help to hold the plants in place a small strip of lead can be folded round each stem where it emerges from the gravel.

This lead must not be put on too tightly or it will interfere with plant growth.

With the planting done the tank can be topped up with water to the level of the bottom edge of the top horizontal angle-iron strip of the tank, and the heater and thermostat should be switched on.

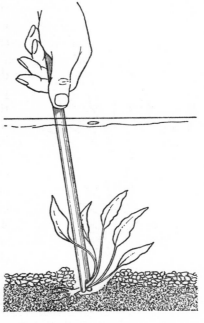

The tank cover, together with its electric light bulb, should be stood on top of the tank and the light switched on. As there must be a certain amount of condensation inside the cover, it is a good idea to wrap black adhesive tape round the bulb holder to prevent moisture getting to the contacts.

Patience now comes into play for the tank must be allowed seven to ten days to settle down. At the end of this time the water temperature should be keeping steady somewhere between the 70°F to

Using forked stick for planting out

74°F (21°C to 23°C) mark, and the plants should be looking perfectly healthy.

Apart from anything absolutely essential (such as adjustment of the thermostat or the replacement of plants that may have drifted free of the gravel) the tank must be left undisturbed during this settling down period. It is possible that the water may appear cloudy soon after the tank has been set up but it should clear itself at the end of about seven days.

With the tank thus arranged and the settling down period having passed, everything is ready for the introduction of the fish into the tank, in the way described in the chapter on buying and transporting the stock.

It might be convenient at this stage to raise the question of water snails, for they cannot be given a chapter to themselves. If it is decided to make use of them they can be put into the tank at the same time as the fish.

Some snails are reasonably decorative but the main reason for putting them in the tank is that they will act as scavengers and eat some of the waste food before it has had a chance to rot.

In fact, the scavenging abilities of snails are often overrated. It can even be argued that the waste products for which they are responsible (which have to be removed with other rubbish to keep the tank clean) almost equals the amount of waste food that they eat.

Strip of lead round stem to hold plant in place.

Snails breed fairly quickly and if the food in the tank is insufficient or not to their taste, they are quite likely to feed off the plants. It is easy enough to get rid of the excess snail population but whereas they were once thought to be almost essential, there has been, for some time past, a change of heart among fish-keepers and many refuse to have them.

Under no circumstances can snails be put into breeding tanks as they are remarkably fond of fish eggs.

If it is decided that a couple of water snails will add interest to the tank the variety known as the red or scarlet 'ramshorn' is cheap, easy to buy, and quite decorative.

Red or scarlet ramshorn snail

4

Breeds of Tropical Fish

ALTHOUGH some thought will have been given to the species of fish that will be kept even before the tank has been set up, this chapter lists the characteristics of some of the more common tropical fish in alphabetical order.

This list should be useful for reference, though relatively only a few species are described. To draw up a full list would need a chapter several times the length of this and the result would be of little value to most fish-keepers.

A word about fish names might be helpful.

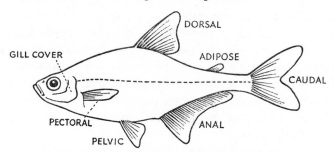

Diagram of fish showing arrangement of fins

Most fish have a widely accepted 'common' name though in some cases there is also an alternative name. For example, the 'guppy' is sometimes called the 'rainbow' or 'millions' fish, and the 'beacon' is also known as the 'head and tail light' fish.

The number of distinct species that can be classed as tropical fish runs into thousands, and tropical fish keeping is a world-wide hobby. In this country the common names are, of course, in English, but overseas the name will be in the local language. The English and (say) German names for one particular species of fish need not be the same, even in translation.

Foreign names need cause no concern. Yet even in English-language magazines words are used, such as 'characins', 'carps', etc., which may be puzzling to the beginner.

Earlier it was stated that, as far as possible, scientific terms would be avoided, but it is necessary to touch on this subject.

A scientist must be precise and cannot risk confusion by using common names, however well understood they may be in his own country. He uses a nomenclature based on Latin and Greek because these are the international languages of science.

On differences in breeding habits, body formation and other characteristics the scientist classifies fish into 'orders', 'sub-orders' and 'families'. These sub-divisions are given titles such as Cyprinidae and Characidae, though a more popular name is also given. Thus, a fish can be said to be a member of the 'carp', 'characin', 'catfish', 'loach' or other family.

Breeding habits are important, so a fish may be described as a 'live-bearer' or 'egg-layer' according to the way in which the young are produced. More will be said about this later, but these descriptions are only popular alternatives for a scientific classification.

Having divided fish into families the scientist gives every type a two-part scientific name. The first part of the name gives what we may call the 'breed' of the fish, and the second part the special 'variety' of that breed.

Thus, many of the fish commonly called 'tetras' have the first name of *Hyphessobrycon*, and this is followed by '*gracilis*,' '*pulchripinnis*' or other 'specific epithet'.

Naturally most people prefer to use the name 'neon tetra' rather than *Hyphessobrycon innesi*, but scientific names may be found helpful on occasions. When a breed is first put on the market it may be under a scientific name which it keeps for several months, or even years, until acquiring a popular name. The scientific name often gives a good indication of the type of fish to expect.

Many fish-keepers avoid scientific names for their fish but are happy to use at least part of such a name when dealing with water plants (e.g. *Vallisneria*).

If scientific names are learned gradually they may prove useful but the novice must not be frightened of them. As this is a beginner's book scientific names have not been given, except where there is no generally accepted common name.

A list of scientific names for some of the more popular tropical species has been given in an appendix, but there is a point that needs explaining.

As scientific knowledge increases and more facts are known the scientific name may be changed, so that in one book the 'checkered barb' may be described as *Barbus oligolepis*, while in another it is called *Puntius oligolepis*. It is usually only the 'breed' name that alters, and cases are on record of a breed being given a scientific name which, later, was altered, and, later again, reverted to the original name.

These alternative breed names are described as 'synonyms' and there are many reasons why different writers prefer one title to another. In general, of course, the latest agreed scientific name is more likely to be found in periodicals than in books in hard-back covers, for the names may be changed while the latter are still on sale.

The beginner may find synonyms, as well as alternative common names, to be rather confusing, but if he is really interested they will soon be recognised for what they are.

American flag fish (Plate 16)   This is sometimes called the 'flag fish', and is green in colour with many rows of red dots; the adult grows to a maximum size of about 2½ in. (6·35 cm).

Both sexes have a short bar passing vertically through the eye and a black spot behind the gill covers. The male is of more attractive appearance than the female, the anal, caudal and dorsal fins being marked with dotted red bands.

The fish prefer a diet containing plenty of vegetable matter, but should not be fed exclusively on this.

Angel fish (Plates 3 and 24)   A popular species best kept in quantities of four or more as they prefer to cruise in company. The background colour is yellow to olive-green but is barred with stripes almost, if not completely, black. The circular body outline is very distinctive. Although peaceable, large specimens should not be put in with tiny breeds, and for a mixed tank a body size of slightly more than 1¼ in. (3 cm) should be regarded as the maximum.

Angel fish thrive on live foods but prefer frequent changes of diet. When the fish are out of condition or badly frightened the distinctive bars lose their colour.

Aphyocypris pooni (Plate 9)   This fish is often sold as the white cloud mountain minnow (see below), but it is not the true fish of that name. It is of almost identical appearance, but can be distinguished by the narrow blue border on the dorsal fin. As almost always, the male is more brilliantly coloured than the female. Treatment of the fish is the same as for the true white cloud.

Argentine pearl (Plate 13)   Unlike most tropicals, these Argentine 'killifishes' find their natural home in somewhat brackish water, and the two sexes are so different in colouring that they might be mistaken for different breeds.

The female is of a greenish body colouring, with irregular vertical stripes of deep brown; the underside of the mouth is of a greyish-blue tint. The male is of a much darker shade of green and displays regularly spaced white dots both on the body and fins. All fins are edged in black, the anal fin carrying a fairly broad red band. Adult fish have a body length of 3 in. (7·5 cm).

A pair of Argentine pearls add an attractive touch to any aquarium, but unless specialising in the breed it is unwise to keep too many of them, as, when more than one pair is present, they will not always settle down happily in a community tank.

Australian rainbow   A fish showing a considerable range of colour hues, and with a pale red banding in the fins. In the male, anal and dorsal fins are particularly striking.

This is a playful fish that enjoys curving and twisting in the light. It is seen to advantage in small shoals in a tank not too densely planted. No special diet is required and it

Australian rainbow

is not a difficult fish from which to breed. It may grow rather larger than many other tropicals, but is a peaceable species.

Beacon fish (Plate 1)   A small, active breed having golden fins. The body colour varies from olive-green to silver, but there are bright orange markings over eye and tail and a black mark at the base of the latter. The alternative name of 'head and tail light fish' is sometimes used.

Beacon fish have no food preferences and are not a difficult species from which to breed.

Belgian flag tetra (Plate 1)   This South American fish (known as the 'flag' or 'striped tetra') takes its popular name from the three coloured stripes that run from gill to tail, narrowing towards the latter. The red, yellow and black of the flag of the Belgians is re-placed, in the fish, by red, a pale yellow and deep blue.

When fully grown the species measures about $1\frac{3}{4}$ in. (4 cm). The fish are typical tetras, being moderately hardy and looking at their best when kept in a small shoal. The female can be distinguished from the male by her rather fuller body.

Black molly   This is a peaceful live-bearer that sometimes grows to a larger size than the average tropical fish.

With some varieties, the fry are not black at birth but attain a rich black colour as they mature: with others, even the fry are a dull jet black, though the colour appears to take on a velvety sheen as the fish grow older.

Black molly

The breed is not particularly interested in live food and thrives on dried foods, preferring those with a higher vegetable than animal content. Live food should, of course, be fed on occasion.

Black widow (Plate 10)   An egg-layer from South America. The body is greenish with a couple of black lines but the most distinctive feature is the fan-shaped black anal fin, though the blackish colour extends up into the dorsal fin.

31

As the fish ages, the fin colouring becomes rather more mottled, but the deep colour returns at spawning time. Black widows are not fussy about diet, and they thrive better than most fish on dried foods, though they appreciate variety even with this. Scraped raw meat or liver is greatly favoured.

Solitary black widows are likely to become aggressive but in a shoal of their own kind they are peaceable.

Blackline tetra   A true tetra, though it grows to greater body length than the average of the breed. It is silvery in colour with a black line (edged with yellow) running the length of the body. Male and female are similar in appearance but the former is the slimmer of the pair.

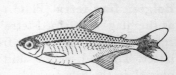

Blackline tetras prefer tanks having plenty of vegetation. They are not

Blackline tetra

fussy as regards diet and are not a difficult species from which to breed.

Bloodfin (Plate 8)   These fish have a greenish-silver body with blood-red fins; they grow to a length of about $1\frac{1}{2}$ in. (3·75 cm). Bloodfins are egg-layers, toothed, and have an adipose fin. The species is not demanding as regards diet and does well on most prepared dried foods. The fin colouring is a useful guide to the condition of the fish.

Blue gourami (Plate 7)   May grow to 4 in. long (10 cm). It is of an attractive blue shade with touches of very pale yellow, and with white specks in the fins. The male has a large and distinctive dorsal fin.

The blue gourami needs a large, well-planted tank. In spite of its size it is quite inoffensive. Food requirements are the same as for the other gouramis.

Bronze catfish (Plate 12)   The catfish are bottom feeders and are thus very good scavengers. This particular variety is, for a catfish, rather active but like most of the breed is not very handsome. It does not grow to too large a size for the community tank, and is of a dark bronze colour, with a white patch beneath the mouth. Like all catfishes, this has the typical 'whiskers' (barbels) above the mouth.

Brown acara (Plates 6 and 24)   This species (*Aequidens portalegrensis*) has also been described as the green acara, and there is also a closely related species sold as the blue acara. It is a larger fish than most of the tropicals and has been known to grow to a length of almost 6 in. (15 cm). The body colour is green but the edges of the scales are edged with brown. Like most of the cichlid family the head is large, and this species has dark brown eyes.

The dorsal fin is large and of attractive shape; the fins of the female are smaller and less pointed than those of the male.

Bumble bee (Plate 7)   The name gives a good description of this fish, which is distinctively marked with gold and black bands. It does not grow to a large size, rarely exceeding 1½ in. (3·75 cm) in length, and is exceedingly active. The bumble bee prefers a higher water temperature than do most tropical fish, but it is not fussy as regards diet.

Cardinal tetra   The cardinal tetra closely resembles the popular neon tetra in appearance, but is of larger size. It is a peaceful member of the community tank but should be kept in a shoal of at least four to six. Body length may reach 1½ in. (3·75 cm). An immature cardinal can be distinguished from the neon in that the red stripe is continuous down the entire length of the body.

Cardinal tetra

Checkered barb   This is a fish that must be kept with its own kind or it will develop into a bully. It grows to about 1½ in. (3·75 cm) and is of a brown (or, in the male, definitely copper) colour. The fins of the male are edged with black.

The breed prefers to swim towards the bottom of the tank, which must be well planted. It is not fussy as regards food, but an occasional live meal is appreciated.

Checkered barb

33

Cherry barb (Plate 9)   One of the most popular and prettiest barbs. The male is golden-yellow on top, with a black band running down the body and across the tail fin. The rest of this, all other fins, and the body below the banding is of cherry-red.

The fish is placid except when he takes his exercise in the company of his own species. It is not an easy fish from which to breed.

Clown barb (Plate 5)   The clown barb is usually to be seen rooting about at the bottom of the tank, and being a vigorous, rather large, fish, it may cause some damage if the plants are not well rooted.

The background colour is pale yellow; there is a large blue spot on the centre of the body, and a blue line runs from this to a small blue spot immediately in front of the tail. The body shows other blue spots and markings, while all fins are pale pink.

The clown barb does best on a diet that has a high percentage of live food.

Diamond tetra   A South American fish that is a useful member of the community tank, having a body length of some $2\frac{1}{2}$ in. (6·75 cm). The fins are reddish-brown, the dorsal of the male being crescent shaped, and the anal deep; the fins of the female are less prominent.

The fish is of a silvery background colour, with small blue and green spots and occasional patches of gold. The body is fairly deep, but rather arched throughout the length.

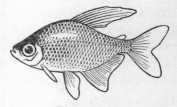

Diamond tetra

There is nothing unusual about the care or maintenance of the fish.

Dwarf gourami (Plate 20)   The female is mauve or greenish and drab in appearance when compared with the male, the characteristic bands being somewhat lacking in colour. In the male, alternate bars of bluish-green and red, running vertically across the body, are prominent. The dorsal and anal fins are unusually long.

The species grows to an average length of 1½ in. (3·75 cm) and is the smallest of the gourami breed.

This is not a fussy feeder, but it relishes a meal of insect larvae. The dwarf gourami is an easy species from which to breed.

Dwarf rainbow cichlid   The fish takes its name from the fantastic range of colours that it can display, and which are continually changing. The anal fin is particularly striking, but the caudal fin may also be boldly splashed with colour.

It is unwise to keep more than a single pair in a community tank as they tend to keep to one particular part of the tank, and to chase

Dwarf rainbow cichlid

off all intruders. They do well on normal diets, but are very apt to uproot plants that are not firmly anchored.

Egyptian mouth-breeder (Plate 11)   The fish is one of strange breeding habits. The eggs are laid in a shallow depression in the sand, then the female carries them around in her mouth until they hatch out. Even the tiny fry will seek refuge in the mother's mouth if they scent danger.

The head of the fish is large, and the body brownish-yellow to blue but heavily splashed with blotches of various colours, the fins having green and blue markings; the dorsal fin is very long. As always, the male is more vividly coloured than the female.

Emperor tetra   The fish takes its description from its vivid colouring rather than its size, for when fully grown it measures only 2 in. (5 cm) long. It is not a common fish, but its 'courtship dance' and fin display during the breeding season makes it worthy of a place in any tank. In the male the back and underparts are olive coloured, the sides being bluish with a poorly defined

Emperor tetra

reddish streak. A short spike extends from the caudal fin of the male.

Feather-fin (Plate 8)   This is a hardy little fish that originated in South America, and is one that is better able to withstand a fairly wide range of water temperatures than are most tropicals.

The fins are of a pinkish-brown colour, but the fish takes its name from the straight black and white lines down the front edge of the dorsal and anal fins. The body tends to be rather deep, and of a silvery colour that darkens to a pale green brown towards the caudal fin; it grows to a length of some 2 in. (5 cm).

The feather-fin is not a fussy eater, and does well on packaged foods, though it must be given an occasional live meal. It is an easy species from which to breed and is reasonably long lived.

Firemouth cichlid   The name is taken from the vivid red colouring at the mouth and throat. Anal and dorsal fins are semi-transparent, pointed and very long. Although rarely growing more than 3 in. (7·5 cm) in length the breed can, under very favourable conditions grow to nearly twice that size. The body colour is greyish, but the scales are red rimmed; there may

Firemouth cichlid

be some vertical bands of darker colour on the body.

The firemouth is apt to be quarrelsome on occasion, and some fish-keepers confine them to tanks of their own breed. They like to root round the bottom of plants, which therefore need to be well anchored. A large, well-planted tank is advisable.

Five-banded barb   A rather timid fish that prefers to keep close to plants and rocks, and which should be given plenty of hiding places in the tank. It is not a species that stands up well to rapid changes in the water temperature.

One of the bright blue vertical bands passes through the eye and another close to the tail. The body colour is brownish, with a reddish

Five-banded barb

PLATE 9 · (*Natural size*)

1 & 2. White cloud mountain minnow.   3 & 4. Cherry barb.
5 & 7. *Aphyocypris pooni*, female.   6. *Aphyocypris pooni*, male.

PLATE 10
Black widow.

PLATE 11
Egyptian mouth-
breeder.

PLATE 12 · (*Natural size*)

1. Bronze catfish.   2. Leopard catfish.   3. Spotted catfish.

tinge, the edges of the scales being fringed with yellow. The dorsal fin may have a red streak. A body length of 2 in. (5 cm) is about average for a fully grown adult.

Flame fish (Plate 1)   Sometimes called the flame tetra or red tetra, this little fish grows to more than 1½ in. (3·75 cm) long. It is reasonably hardy, active, and a good community tank fish.

All the fins of the breed are red and are edged with black, except for the caudal and dorsal. The flame fish is red beneath, except for a silvery patch below the head, the back being olive green. Just behind the gill covers are two short dark vertical bars.

Although the flame fish will do quite well on dried foods, it must be given an occasional live meal to keep it in the pink of condition.

Flying barb   A slender fish, with the dorsal fin set well back towards the tail. It has two pairs of barbels, one pair being exceptionally long. A double line extends down the length of the body, this being golden yellow above and brown beneath. Above and below the double line the body colour is greenish. The male is recognisable

Flying barb

from the female by the greater distinctness of the coloured lines.

The flying barb keeps towards the top of the tank, and is not particularly fussy as regards diet.

Giant danio   An active fish that sometimes grows to a length in excess of 4 in. (10 cm).

The breed is of a bluish background colour with a yellow striping that leaves a broad, central blue band. In the male this band con-

Giant danio

tinues across the tail, but with the female the band turns upwards before reaching that point.

Like all danios this species is undemanding as regards food and is easy to breed.

Glowlight tetra   One of the true tetras, growing to a body length greater than most of the breed, but still a small fish.

This species has a bright orange spot over and near the eye, and a broken band of the same colour extending to the base of the tail; the same colour is also found at the front of the dorsal fin in many specimens. The body colour is green and gold.

Glowlight tetra

No tetra species is exceptionally hardy but this is perhaps the hardiest of the breed.

Glowlights need nothing special for food or tank conditions though they like plenty of vegetation in the tank. They are at their best in small shoals.

Guppy (Plate 17)   Without doubt this live-bearer is the most popular of all tropical fish with beginners, as it is strong, active, and able to withstand temperature variations, etc., that would kill off other species.

It would be difficult to find two males identical in appearance. Green, red, blue and yellow body colour, with blotches or spots of other colours distinguish the male from the plain grey or yellow female, and there are also variations in fin shaping, etc. The female is larger than the male, the latter usually being just over 1 in. (2·5 cm) long.

Guppies are always readily available and are the cheapest tropical fish. A tank containing nothing but guppies can be set up and to the layman it will seem to contain several different breeds. Moreover, guppies breed readily and may increase the tank population without the owner even noticing it until the fry have matured.

The names of 'rainbow' and 'millions' fish have sometimes been given to the breed.

Harlequin fish (Plate 4)   Since its introduction this has always been a popular fish. The most distinctive feature is the black triangle at the base of the tail. The front of the body is silvery, but is brownish-green at the back up to the dorsal fin where the colour changes to rose-pink and curves down to the black triangle. It normally grows to just under 2 in. (5 cm) in length. The dorsal and front part of the tail fin are reddish-brown. This is an egg-laying species but not one from which breeding is easy. The harlequin fish is undemanding as regards diet.

Headstander (Plate 14)   As far as food is concerned this is a bottom feeder and is therefore useful as a scavenger. The reason for the common name of the fish is obvious, and its 'acrobatics' can be quite amusing.

The headstander is not a colourful fish, the body being greenish-brown with small, darker spots and a dark line along the body. It grows to 3 in. (7·5 cm) or more in length, but in spite of its size it is peaceable enough for the community tank. The breed likes a well-planted tank and, in spite of its habits, it does not cause as much damage to the plants as some of the other bottom feeders.

Jack Dempsey (Plate 21)   To a small tropical fish the Jack Dempsey with its deep body, massive-looking head and size (sometimes approaching 6 in. (15 cm) must seem a rather fearsome sight. Yet the fish is peaceful enough, though it is probably at its best in a tank confined to its own breed.

The background colour is a deep brown, darkening almost to black as the fish gets older, but it carries a regular marking of dark blue spots that lighten in colour towards the top of the body, becoming almost yellow. The marking is continued in the fins, which are of attractive shape and size. The eyes are in keeping with the size of the head.

The Jack Dempsey loves to browse round the bottom of the plants, and its size is such that it is likely to uproot them. Feeding and maintenance of the fish are along the usual lines.

Jewel cichlid (Plate 21)   This is a nest-building cichlid of handsome appearance, but rather shallower in the body than most others of the breed; it is sometimes called the 'red cichlid'.

One of the noticeable points about this breed is that on each side of the body there are two large dark spots, one halfway between tail and gills, and one just behind the latter; the male is dark greenish above and orange beneath, whereas the female tends to be reddish along the back, but in both cases the body is sprinkled with blue spots. The fins are of good shape and attractive colour.

While not growing as large as some of the cichlids, the jewel can, on occasion, develop into a bully, so he needs some watching in the community tank.

Kissing gourami (Plate 15)   The name comes from the manner in which the fish appear to purse up their lips when approaching others of the same breed.

The male and female are difficult to distinguish. The body tends to be squat, greenish above and very pale lilac below, with faint horizontal striping. Fins are clear, with a faint banding in the dorsal and anals, being most prominent in the former.

Although not really aggressive the kissing gourami sometimes gives that impression, although other breeds ignore its threatening gestures. It has no special requirements but prefers food that is rich in vegetable matter.

The kissing gourami needs plenty of swimming room to display itself when mature.

Lemon tetra   The basic colouring is yellow, though the anal and front of the dorsal fin are edged with black. The female is slightly the larger of the pair.

Being true tetras these fish look best when kept in small shoals; they tend to cruise around in the lower half of the tank. They do not need anything special as regards diet or tank conditions. If not bullied

Lemon tetra

by larger breeds lemon tetras settle down well in a mixed tank.

Leopard catfish (Plate 12)   This is one of the true catfishes and has always been regarded as one of the most handsome of the breed. It has all the normal catfish habits of scavenging, etc., but it is one of the best of the cats for the community tank.

The leopard catfish does not grow to any great size, rarely exceeding $2\frac{1}{2}$ in. (6·75 cm) in length. The body is handsomely splotched, with three black stripes on each side running almost the entire length of the body; there is a splash of brownish-yellow around the eye. All the fins are attractively marked, the dorsal displaying a large black patch near the tip.

An occasional live meal is appreciated by the leopard cat, although it may not be easy to ensure that the fish feeding at the top of the tank do not get the lion's share before the food is low enough for the leopard!

Liberty molly (Plate 16)   There is a world of difference between the black molly and this fish, which is sometimes called the green molly.

The liberty molly's body is various shades of green, but silvery beneath, though at times the green colour tends to develop a blue tint. Fins are brightly coloured and outlined with a band, commonly of orange, but the dorsal, in particular, is smaller than with most mollies.

This is an excellent community fish. It needs no special care but when giving powdered foods remember that it prefers one that has a high vegetable content.

Lined panchax (Plate 16)   This is a killifish from India and Ceylon that may grow to a length of 4 in. (10 cm). It is a breed that prefers to remain near the top of the tank. The fish has had many changes in its scientific name and is known to some fish-keepers as *Panchax lineatus* and to others as *Apocheilus lineatus*. The alternative name of striped panchax is also used for the breed.

The fish is slender-bodied, carrying regular rows of white spots, some occasional red dots and vertical bands of darkish green. The anal fin is long and the dorsal is set well back towards the caudal, all three fins carrying red markings.

Lyre-tail (Plate 13)   A glance at the coloured plate will show what a really attractive fish the lyre-tail is, for it is not only the body shape and finnage that appeal but also the glorious colouring.

It is only the male that has the lyre-shaped caudal fin. The body colour is yellowish-green with dark red stripes and blotches in the male, while the female is a pale shade of brown, with reddish spots. Anal and dorsal fins are marked with maroon and blue, while the pelvic and pectoral fins are reddish or orange with a few white spots.

Neon tetra (Plate 1)   The most distinctive feature is the blue-green streak running along the body, for this has a fluorescent quality that has given the fish its name. The rear half of the body beneath the streak is an attractive, glowing red. Adult fish rarely exceed 1 in. (2·5 cm) in length.

Neons are extremely active and do well in a mixed tank. They require nothing special in the way of food or treatment but should always be kept in small shoals.

Neon tetras are egg-layers but they are difficult to breed successfully.

Nigger barb (Plates 5 and 19)   This fish is rather unusual in that it prefers to browse towards the bottom of the tank. It is smaller than some other barbs and it also differs from them in that the bars tend to merge into each other as the fish grows older.

The young fish is of a uniform silvery colour, with clearly marked vertical bars. In the adult fish the entire back part of the body appears to be black while the head and front part of the underside develop a reddish tint.

Nigger barbs do well on a diet of dried food if it has a high vegetable content, though they may be fed an occasional meal of white worms. Like the rest of the family, the nigger barbs love to nibble at aquarium plants. They do not like a recently set-up tank but thrive in one in which the water has matured over a period of time before they are introduced to it.

Although active, nigger barbs are peaceable and good members of the mixed tank.

One-striped pencil fish (Plate 8)   With this breed it is extremely important that the food given is only of small size, as the fish have tiny mouths.

The fish is very slender, likes a thickly planted tank, and always swims at an angle, head upwards. It is silvery in colour (sometimes with a slightly greenish tinge) with a distinctive black stripe running the whole length of the body, with a splash of colour on the caudal fin. The lower part of the tail fin is larger than the upper segment.

The one-striped pencil fish gives a touch of novelty to every tropical tank, not only because of the position in which it swims but also because its languid meandering around the tank is in sharp contrast to the quick, darting movements of most other breeds.

Otocinclus catfish   Like all catfish this prefers to remain towards the bottom of the tank, and is constantly nibbling at the plants.

It is a rather slender fish, with a long, pointed head. It is of a pale olive-green colour above, with a slightly darker band running the length of the body. Beneath the band the colour is an extremely pale

Otocinclus catfish

yellow, fading into white. Fins are almost colourless but there are a couple of dark markings across the tail.

The catfish roots round the bases of the plants, usually without causing damage. The breed grows to some 2 in. (5 cm) in length. It does not do well on an exclusive diet of dried food and if possible should be fed chiefly on live food, with an occasional vegetable meal.

The species does not always travel well though after a few days in a new tank it should come back to peak condition.

Paradise fish (Plate 20)   A bubble-nesting breed, growing to 3 in. (7.5 cm) in length, that is often amazingly beautiful, more especially during the breeding season.

The most noticeable markings are the alternate bands of blue or green and scarlet. The fins, however, are also of distinctive shape, having an orange tint, with occasional white spots in the caudal fin, but the anal and dorsal fins show the same colours as the body.

The paradise fish will sometimes be seen on the surface of the water, apparently gulping air. This is not a sign that the fish is really suffering from lack of oxygen, but is a characteristic of the breed.

Pearl danio (Plate 4)   An alert and active fish, growing to a maximum size of about 2 in. (5 cm).

Under aquarium lighting the fish seems as if its body is of mother of pearl, usually having a violet tinge that enhances the effect. There is another species (the golden pearl danio) similar in all respects, but with the body showing a yellowish (almost golden) tinge.

This is one of the easiest of fish to maintain, being hardy and undemanding as regards diet. Like most members of the family it does well on dried foods and likes browsing on the aquatic plants.

The activity of the pearl danio can be annoying to more placid fish, but it is a very popular species with most aquarists.

Pearl gourami (Plate 20)   This fish is also known as 'lace gourami'. It originated in the Malay Peninsula, and may grow to a length of 5 in. (12·5 cm), or even more.

The background colour of the fish is greyish-blue, but it is flecked with white and blue, giving a pearly appearance. During the breeding season the male develops a deep red colour on the breast, and he has a better shaped and larger dorsal fin. The pectoral and dorsal fins are in varying shades of red.

The pearl gourami is a peaceful fish for the community tank. It prefers a diet that is rich in vegetable matter, but it is small mouthed and can take only tiny particles of food.

Platy (Plate 17)   A small fish, rarely exceeding 1 in. (2·5 cm) in length, and popular with all fish-keepers but especially so with breeders. All platys will interbreed and they are often used as the stock for developing new strains.

Among the more common varieties the golden wagtail, red and gold platys may be mentioned.

The golden wagtail has a black tail and fins with the body of a golden colour, but in the gold platy the fins are of the same colour as the body. In some cases there may be a touch of colour in the dorsal fin of the golden wagtail. Specimens that show this fin colouring are not as highly regarded as those that have the uniform black

44

fins. The red variety should have a uniform red colour throughout.

The platys are peaceful but active. Although appreciating an occasional change of diet they do quite well on dried foods, but they like a well-planted tank so that they can nibble at the vegetation.

Pompadour fish (Plates 22 and 24) This can be called a moody fish, because its colour changes according to its state of health and the conditions in the tank.

The body is almost circular. The colour is a green to a brownish shade, with eight vertical bars, not all of which can be clearly seen because they are almost blotted out by blue and green lines that develop during the breeding season. Fins are somewhat reddish but are marked with blue and greenish-gold, though the caudal fin may be pale green.

Although sometimes an expensive fish, this is one well worth keeping in the community tank. It should be fed almost exclusively on live food.

Red rivulus (Plate 13) There are several varieties of *Rivulus*, all very similar in appearance and usually sold by dealers as rivulus, plain and simple.

This particular variety (*Rivulus urophthalmus*) has a yellow body marked with closely spaced rows of red spots. The body is very slim, with the caudal fin roundish in shape, and the anal and dorsal fins set back close to the caudal. The fins are grey in colour, red spots being visible on the dorsal and anal fins in the male. A body length of $2\frac{1}{2}$ in. (6·5 cm) is average for a fully grown adult.

The rivulus is not an unfriendly fish and does not need anything special in the way of food.

Red-tailed black shark (Plate 15) The 'sharks', of which there are several different varieties, take their name from the body shape, and they came originally from Thailand and Indo-China. They are all very similar, apart from the colour of the fins, but the red-tailed black shark has proved most popular for the tropical tank. This is an egg-laying breed, shining black with the exception of the caudal fin, which is vivid red.

45

Tropical sharks are best kept in small shoals, as the solitary specimen is liable to 'take over' an area of the tank and develop into a bully. They grow to a size of 4½ in. (12 cm) or more, and accordingly need to be moved into a special tank as they grow more mature. While young they may be kept in a mixed tank, to which they will add a distinct touch of colour.

These fish have a strong preference for a vegetable diet, and are constantly nibbling at plants and algae. They swim very slowly but if angered they are capable of developing a high turn of speed.

Red-throated panchax (Plate 16)   A small fish (2½ in. or 6 cm long) of attractive colouring that can stand up to a wide range of water temperatures.

The male can be distinguished from the female by a red patch on the underside of the mouth. Fins are a brownish-yellow in both sexes, but those of the male are edged with black. Bars of dark colour surround the lower part of the body, which is of a paler colour than the brown back. The caudal fins may be flecked with dark brown spots.

All fish of this breed need careful watching as they can develop into bullies. This particular species is, perhaps, the least objectionable in that respect.

Rosy barb (Plates 5 and 18)   This is one of the smaller of the popular barbs, but is active and alert, and quite peaceful. A growth in excess of 2 in. (5 cm) is most unusual.

Adult males are of a coppery colour, and have the anal, ventral and dorsal fins edged with black; the rosy-red colour is most prominent when the fish is in a breeding condition. The female is a silvery colour but somewhat darker on the back, and both these and the males have a black spot close to the tail.

These fish should not be introduced into a newly set-up tank. They take any food with relish but are inveterate plant nibblers, which indicates that a vegetable diet is particularly appreciated. They do best in the company of their own kind; they are hardy, and the species is easy to breed from.

Rosy tetra (Plate 1)   Sometimes known as the black flag fish, this is a true tetra and is peaceful, so it is well suited to the community tank. Its maximum length when fully adult is about 2 in. (5 cm).

In colour, the body is pinkish, but towards the tail the colour is darker. The dorsal fin is black with a white edging towards the front, and, in the case of the female, has a vivid red patch towards the top of the fin. Anal and pelvic fins have white tips, though these may have a slight yellowish hue.

As with all fish of this breed the rosy tetra is at its best when kept in a small shoal.

Sailfin molly   A species that needs a fair amount of space for swimming if it is to be seen to its best advantage. The fish is of a silvery colour with dark spots, but slightly yellow towards the front underside of the body, with a large dorsal fin edged with yellow. There are numerous small dots on the blue and orange caudal fin.

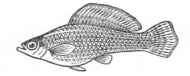
Sailfin molly

This particular breed must have plenty of vegetable matter in its diet. It is a live-bearing breed that grows to a good size, though its nature is quite a peaceful one.

Siamese fighter   In spite of his name and reputation the Siamese fighter is a peaceable enough fish – until he meets a male of his own breed. He can even be made to attack his own reflection by placing a mirror against the side of the tank. Once fighting starts it continues until one of the males is badly hurt, or possibly killed. The survivor will have suffered serious damage and even if his wounds heal, his fins will never return to their original glory.

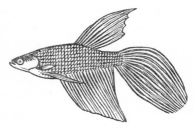
Siamese fighter

The female is quite peaceful and does not fight.

47

As is commonly the case the male is the handsomer of the two sexes, having a general body colouring of light blue or red. He is also distinguished by a high dorsal fin and a long anal fin.

The species is an egg-laying one and can be bred in an aquarium tank. Only one male can, of course, be kept in a tank at any one time. There are no special requirements as regards food.

Silver hatchet These fish spend most of their time at the top of the tank. Under natural conditions they live almost entirely on insect life, so in the tank their diet must consist largely of live food. The hatchets are surface skimmers and often try to leap from the water, but they tame down admirably for life in the community tank. With no live insects flying above the water to attract their attention their jumping habit is less important.

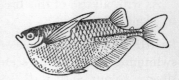

Silver hatchet

This particular species is hardy and active, with a thin body of the peculiar shaping that has given the fish its common name. The body colouring is yellowish with a distinct silvery sheen, and a faint, darker stripe runs down the centre of the body. The pectoral fins are particularly noticeable, being long and of unusual shape. There is little difference between the sexes in appearance.

Several varieties of hatchet fish are available, including the marbled hatchet, which is also suitable for the tropical tank.

Sleeper fish (Plate 23) This is of the same family of fishes as the bumble bee described earlier, but it lacks the colour and agility of that fish. It may grow to be $3\frac{1}{2}$ in. (9 cm) long when fully adult, but it is a difficult fish from which to breed.

The body colour is mottled brown and grey, but a few blue spots can be seen. Male and female cannot be distinguished easily. The fins are not particularly prominent as regards either size or shape, but they may, with the exception of the caudal, be edged in blue.

This breed needs a large and well-planted tank. It will thrive if it is fed mainly on live food.

Splashing tetra   A slender fish with fins of attractive shape, the male growing to a length of 3 in. (7·5 cm), with the female some ½ in. (1·25 cm) shorter. The scales are large and edged in a dark colour so that the brownish-green body seems to be covered with a gridwork of fine lines. The dorsal fin shows a black patch, the fin colouring being yellow, but fading into red at the

Splashing tetra

edges. The upper part of the caudal fin is larger and more elaborately shaped than the lower. The female fish is less colourful than the male.

The splashing tetra is active but peaceful, and gets along quite well on normal diets. The breed is most unusual in that its eggs are laid completely out of the water.

Spotted catfish (Plate 12)   Known also as the peppered catfish, this is an excellent scavenger, but has a fault typical of the breed: it will root up any plant that is not firmly anchored.

The body colour is dull yellow to greyish-green, the colour usually getting darker towards the caudal fin; it is, however, marbled in white, blue and darker shades of yellow. The barbels are not very long. Fins are of normal size and shape, and the fish, overall, cannot be said to be of good appearance, so is kept by most fish-keepers more for its use than its looks.

The spotted catfish prefers a live diet, but in the community tank this presents some problems. Tubifex worms, etc., that have escaped the fish higher in the tank are likely to burrow in the aquarium gravel, which encourages the catfish to plough up the sand in search of the worms. It may be interesting to note that this, like all true catfishes, depends on taste and smell to find its food, rather than on eyesight.

Spotted danio (Plate 4)   This fish resembles the popular 'zebra' but the banding is dark and the two bottom bars are broken so that they are arranged in a series of spots. The body colouring between the banding is a golden yellow which is of a lighter shade on the underside of the body.

The spotted danio is an active fish and usually does well in a mixed tank.

Although appreciating the occasional meal of white or microworms, the species thrives on dried food, preferring those that have a high vegetable content.

The male and female are not easily distinguishable, though the latter tends to be the slightly fatter of the two. This particular species is said to be the most difficult of the danios from which to breed.

Striped cichlid (Plate 21)   This can be an aggravating fish, for when in perfect health it is colourful and attractive. Loss of colour may not mean that the fish is in poor health, but may even be brought on by a sulking fit. The striped cichlid has the squat body and big head of the Jack Dempsey. The fins are extremely handsome both in colour and shape, being of an orange colour with a patch of blue in the dorsal of the male. In full colouring the front and upper parts of the body are green fading into more of an orange colour on the underparts, and with regular rows of brown spots. With the female the colouring is less vivid and the spots more irregular.

Again, this cichlid is capable of growing to a good size, possibly reaching 5 in. (14 cm) when fully grown. Smaller specimens can be kept in a community tank without trouble.

Sucking catfish   This can develop into an enormous fish, 10 in. (28 cm) or more in length, but it is unlikely to do so under ordinary aquarium conditions. It is regarded as one of the best of the scavengers, particularly where algae are concerned, but it usually prefers to hide itself during the day, and forage for food at night.

Sucking catfish

The sucking catfish is long in the body and has a rather flat head; the mouth is pinkish and large. The colour is grey above and whitish beneath, with brown dots along the side and larger patches of brown towards the head. The dorsal is the only prominent fin, all others seeming small for the size of the fish.

Sucking loach   Again, this fish is favoured more for its use than
its looks, and it closely resembles the sucking catfish in appearance.
The mouth is large and placed lower
down than with most fishes, and with
this mouth the fish can anchor itself
to rocks or the sides of the tank. It
sometimes adopts very strange at-
titudes for swimming, but is active

Sucking loach

and peaceful, though it may eventually reach a length of 5 in.
(13 cm).

When it has cleared a tank of algae, it will be necessary for the fish
to be given food having a high vegetable content, though an
occasional meal of chopped earthworm will be appreciated.

Swordtail (Plate 18)   This is a popular fish with beginners, partly
because it is easy to look after and partly because of the unusual
shaping of the male. The latter has a spike-like projection beneath
the tail, which has been responsible for the name of the breed.

The common varieties are 'red' and 'green' though there may be
variations on these colours. The red swordtail has a body colour of a
deep orange shade while the sword is yellow to orange, with a thin
black line. The green swordtail has a general body colour of green
with a red and yellow line running the length of the body; the tail
matches that of the red swordtail.

These are particularly frisky fish and the males often indulge in
fighting, in which they display more enthusiasm for exercise than a
real desire to inflict damage, although the fins of the contestants may
look rather the worse for wear. They are a live-bearing breed and
may grow (male, including the sword) to a length of nearly 4 in.
(12 cm). The larger specimens are sometimes inclined to bully small
fish of other breeds but if two or more males are kept in a mixed tank
they will tend to ignore the other fish to concentrate on a private feud.

Thick-lipped gourami (Plate 20)   For the community tank
a useful fish that grows only to some 3 in. (7·5 cm) in length, and
which needs no more than ordinary care.

The background colouring is a greyish-yellow, but it is banded with green and a deeper shade of yellow alternately; this banding is liable to colour changes so that the green stripes may be almost red, with the yellow stripes also taking on a reddish tinge. The thick lips from which the fish gets its name are very prominent. In the case of the male fish the dorsal fin is sharply pointed, and this and the anal fin (both of which are very long) are edged with red; the male has a blue patch towards the back of the anal. The fish is unusual, too, in that it has two thread fins that project from beneath the body, these being very thin and red in colour. Other gouramis also show these thread fins.

Three-striped pencil fish (Plate 8)   A handsome slender fish with a body length of 1¾ in. (5·5 cm). It has a broad gold stripe (dotted with red in the male fish) running from nose to tail, with a narrower black stripe above and below this. The underside of the fish is greyish to an almost lilac colour, with the back in various shades of green. The fins are handsomely splashed with red.

This is a quite undemanding fish, needing only the usual care. In conditions of almost complete darkness or very poor light, the fish loses its bands and becomes splotched with red.

Tiger barb (Plate 19)   This is a popular member of the barb family. It grows to about the same size as the rosy barb described earlier.

The body is greenish but the most distinctive feature is the vertical barring. There are four very distinct, black bands. The first bar runs across the eye and the last through the base of the tail. Adult males have patches of red in the fins, apart from the dorsal fin which is black, with a red edging at the rear.

Feeding and water requirements are the same as for the rosy barb. This is not an easy species from which to breed and the parents must be removed immediately after spawning. Tiger barbs prefer to be in small shoals.

Two-spot barb (Plate 5)   The spots from which the fish takes its

PLATE 13 · (*Natural size*)

1. Lyre-tail.   2. Red rivulus.
3 & 4. Argentine pearl, female and male.

PLATE 14

Headstanders.

PLATE 15

(*above*) Red-tailed black shark.
(*below*) Kissing gouramis.

PLATE 16 · (*Natural size*)

1. Red-throated panchax. 2. American flag fish.
3. Liberty molly. 4. Lined panchax.

name are at the base of the tail (this being very prominent) and behind the gills. The body is greenish along the back but silvery or silvery-red down the sides: the red colour deepens as the fish approaches breeding condition. The male can be recognised by the broad band of red at the top of the dorsal, the rest of this fin, and all others, being yellow.

The two-spot barb is lively and hardy. It is also sufficiently good tempered to make a useful community tank fish. Live food is appreciated more than dried, but earthworms, etc., must be chopped very finely as the breed has only a small gullet.

White cloud mountain minnow (Plate 9)   A fish of small growth habit which, when young, rather resembles a neon tetra. The basic body colouring is silvery (with red patches on top of the body and towards the back), the fins being yellow with a red marking in the dorsal.

This is a peaceable species, very active, and needing no special attention as regards diet. Mountain minnows are extremely hardy, able to bear extremes of temperature without much discomfort, and can be bred successfully. They originated in China.

X-ray fish (Plate 8)   A tropical fish in which the colours are more gradually blended than in most other species.

An unusual feature is the white tip to the ventral and anal fins, which are also marked with black. The body colour is silvery and brown, with the tail of a yellowish shade, though it has a tinge of red.

The name of the fish is misleading, as it is far less transparent than some other breeds. Adult fish attain a length of about 1 in. (2·5 cm). It is an egg-laying fish that adjusts well to life in a mixed tank, and is hardy and undemanding as regards food.

It is a peaceable species but looks best when kept in a small shoal, as the fish always cruise in company.

Zebra fish (Plate 4)   A popular fish with a length that rarely exceeds 1 in. (2·5 cm) when fully grown.

The colouring is not that usually thought of as being 'zebra', for the stripes are not black and white and they run horizontally from head to tail. The bars are of yellow and violet alternately, and the anal fin also carries violet coloured bands.

Zebra fish look their best if seven or eight are put in a tank, as they tend to cruise around in shoals. Normally they swim along quite steadily, but are capable of making sudden darts that add considerably to the activity within the tank. They are not fussy feeders and are quite hardy.

Zebra fish are a peaceable breed.

5

Buying and Moving Tropical Fish

WITH some idea of the possible field of choice, the problem of stocking the tank with fish must now be considered.

It would be as well to see how such stock is acquired by the beginner.

This is usually done in one of three ways: (1) by buying or being given surplus fish by other tropical fish-keepers; (2) by buying fish from local water-life stores; (3) by buying from dealers who advertise in the magazines devoted to the hobby. In this third case the fish may have to travel a considerable distance before arriving at their destination.

The first method is the cheapest but may have some disadvantages. It would be a very generous fish-keeper who would give or sell cheaply fish that were first class in every way, and it might be that the only fish to be disposed of would be those the owner thought were not good enough for his own tank. (It might be a different matter if the hobby was being given up.) Again, perhaps unknowingly, the fish disposed of might be sickly and the new owner would find that they died off quickly. This could give an altogether wrong impression about the ease of keeping tropical fish.

It might be a good idea to switch the subject slightly at this point to explain how newly bought stock should be treated to avoid that sort of trouble.

Once a tank has been set up ('established') for some time a new fish should never be put into it until it has spent some time in 'quarantine'. This rule should be observed from whatever source the fish may have come.

The quarantine period should last for a week, and only at the end of that time should a fish that is obviously healthy be transferred to the main tank. Although most tropical fish travel well there are a few

55

breeds that lose condition and look rather poorly after a long train journey, but they soon recover in the quarantine tank. If, at the end of one week in this tank, the fish seems droopy, appears to swim unnaturally, or spends all its time at the bottom of the tank, barely moving, its health is not good and it should not be transferred to the main tank until it has fully recovered.

Ideally, fish should be quarantined in a special tank and, when emptied, this must be thoroughly cleaned and disinfected. This is an

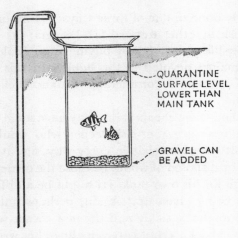

QUARANTINE
SURFACE LEVEL
LOWER THAN
MAIN TANK

GRAVEL CAN
BE ADDED

Quarantine container improvised
from chemistry beaker

important point, for if it is used for sick fish there is always the possibility that disease can be passed on to newly bought, healthy fish that are put into the quarantine tank at some later date.

Because of the extra cost of heaters and tanks, some fish-keepers cannot afford a special quarantine tank.

A useful quarantine tank can be improvised from a thin glass container large enough for the number of fish involved: a chemistry beaker or something similar is usually suitable for the purpose. Some wire or cord is twisted round the neck of this and arranged so that the beaker can be hooked over the edge of the tank with the greater part of it below the water level in the tank itself.

This device needs to be installed some days before it is taken into use. The water inside the beaker will then have a chance to come up to the temperature in the main tank, the transfer of heat between the two being helped by the thinness of the glass.

When putting the water into the beaker forming the quarantine tank the level should be slightly below that of the water in the main tank. There will be no effective quarantine if the fish can jump from one tank to the other. Lowering the water level in the beaker will help to prevent this, but if the fish seem to be particularly lively, a muslin cover should be put over the beaker to keep the fish in bounds without interfering too much with the air supply.

It should be remembered that the quarantine container needs to have a good, wide mouth, so that plenty of water surface is exposed to the air.

A quarantine tank needs to be kept clean of rotting food particles, etc., so the dip tube will have to be used regularly. A thin layer of gravel may be spread over the bottom of the beaker, though this is not absolutely necessary. Rock-work and plants would be out of place in such a small container.

This routine of keeping newly acquired stock in isolation for a while *must* be taken seriously. As a novice fish-keeper the author once lost all the fish in a tank because a sick specimen was put into it, though it was thought that the fish came from a source that was above suspicion. The lesson was an expensive one, so other beginners should take note.

To return to the problem of stocking the tank.

Buying the fish locally is usually the most satisfactory method for the beginner. If possible a shop that specialises in underwater life should be chosen, as the shopkeeper will have a better knowledge of fish-keeping and its particular requirements than the man who keeps a general pet store. Fish are not always kept under the best possible conditions in retail shops, but the buyer has a chance to judge the quality of the fish for himself and can make his own selection.

For moving the fish from the shop to their tank a big vacuum flask (of the type having a large mouth) is ideal. The fish will be put in the flask in water of the proper temperature, and the water will not begin to lose its heat for several hours.

If the distance from shop to house is short the fish will travel comfortably in a closed tin that has been well wrapped in towelling to prevent the water cooling too rapidly. The vacuum container is the better idea, however, as even if most purchases are made locally the time may come when a trip of several miles may be taken to collect a particularly prized specimen, and for such purposes an ordinary tin will not really be suitable.

As already mentioned, most fish travel well, but it is important to see that the container is large enough for the number of fish that it has to hold, and that when travelling by vehicle the container is stood in such a way that it cannot fall or even vibrate too much. Sufficient water must be in the container to prevent it swirling around and to add to the comfort of the fish.

The fish must be put into the tank with as little fuss as possible. The best method is to put the container under the water level of the main tank, open the lid, and allow the fish to swim out. Care must be taken, when doing this, to ensure that the water in the travelling container does not cause the main tank to overflow.

Buying stock from a dealer some distance away is not recommended for the beginner. Most dealers are honest men, but it is not always easy to arrange for the collection of the fish from a railway station (they are usually forwarded by passenger train in suitable containers), the price for the fish may be high compared to local prices because of the carriage charge, and buying on a printed description alone is not advisable until some experience has been gained. Purchases by mail will, generally, be only for the rare species of fish unobtainable locally.

The three systems described are the ones by which most beginners get their stock. Sometimes the chance arises of buying a complete collection from somebody who is giving up the hobby, or getting surplus stock from a local fish-breeder, but for interest nothing is better than setting up a tank for oneself.

Something is now known about buying and moving the fish, but there are other things to be taken into consideration.

Before rushing out to buy tropical fish it is suggested that a good look be taken round the local water-life shops. From this, one particular breed of fish may be found to have a special appeal, but it is more likely that there will be four or five different varieties that catch the eye.

What really occurs is that a choice is made between a 'specialised' and a 'community' tank. In the first type of tank, fish of one particular breed only are kept, while the community tank holds several different varieties of fish that will live together happily.

For the beginner the community tank is the best, because it is easy to install and maintain, and because it gives an opportunity of studying the habits of different species being kept under identical conditions. Many fish-keepers start with a community tank and later, when interest and experience grows, set up one or more specialised tanks.

There are comparatively few breeds that will not settle down happily in a community tank.

There is one little 'rule' that might be remembered, however. As far as possible (and remembering that different breeds grow to different **sizes**) large fish should not be mixed with small, or a certain amount of bullying may occur. Even when the large fish are quite peaceable the smaller ones may take some time to get over their uneasiness.

If a bully is recognised and his behaviour is seriously affecting the other fish, it is advisable to move him into a tank with occupants better able to stand up to him. A bully can be an absolute pest, and anything that affects the health or happiness of the remaining fish must be considered important.

There is some argument among fish-keepers as to whether young or fully grown fish should be bought.

One point in favour of buying fully grown fish is that they show clearly any defects that might not be noticeable in younger stock.

TROPICAL AQUARIUMS

They are also of breeding age and if an interest is going to be taken in this aspect of tropical fish-keeping it will not be long before results can be expected. Such fish usually cost little more to buy than do the younger ones.

Some people offer two objections to this view. Firstly, the average life of a tropical fish is only a matter of a few years – say from three to seven according to breed and condition. Secondly, it is not a simple matter to estimate a fish's age. It is too easy to buy an over-mature fish that will not live long, and, at the same time, be a target for the ill-temper of younger and more aggressive specimens. An old fish, too, is past its prime for breeding.

On balance younger fish will prove the better buy for the beginner. There is no need to worry unduly about serious defects developing in stock that is apparently healthy, and young fish will soon settle down well in a community tank. Old fish are less likely to be happy in a new tank with new companions.

6

Feeding the Fish

MANY troubles that occur in keeping tropical fish are the direct result of incorrect feeding. The most common mistake is the provision of too much dried food. A high percentage of this falls to the bottom of the tank where it decomposes and affects the purity of the water. In addition to this, incorrect feeding is liable to cause digestive trouble among the stock.

This chapter is concerned with the feeding of adult fish; the food for fry being considered later.

The general rule should be to feed sparingly two or three times a day. The fish should come to their food eagerly, but they do not have the great appetites with which some fish-keepers credit them. More fish die from over-eating than starvation.

Fish foods are divided into 'live' and 'dry'. Both have special virtues and it is a mistake to feed continuously with the one type, or even on the same species of live food. A change of diet can be as effective in keeping a fish in good health as it is with human beings.

Some fish-keepers claim for live food that it cannot rot in the same way as dried foods. This is only partly true, because certain creatures have a short life span in an aquarium and if not eaten within a reasonable time they will die and start to pollute the water. Live food, until eaten, also uses up oxygen. Not every form of live food can be put into the tank in any quantity, so storage of it may be something of a problem.

Fish have their preferences, and although the foods described below are suitable for all tropicals, some kinds will be taken more eagerly than others. The fish-keeper will soon distinguish those foods that his stock particularly relish, and will adjust his feeding systems accordingly.

Dried foods   Dried foods sold as suitable for goldfish and other coldwater breeds are of no use for tropical fish. The manufacturers of pet foods offer a good range of mixtures suitable for tropicals and after a little experimenting one of these will be found very suitable for the particular tank concerned. Such foods are sometimes sold in grains of a special size, intended for fish of particular sizes, but this is unimportant as long as the grains are not too large.

There is one important point about dried foods. However carefully they are mixed and packed there may be some fine food dust in the package. This should not be put into a tank of adult fish. It will only be ignored, fall to the bottom, and rot. There are certain stages in the life of the fry when tiny food grains will be snapped up, so the food dust can be filtered out and kept for the breeding tanks.

When a pinch of dried food is put into the top of the tank it stays there only a short time before sinking. Most fish feed at the top of the tank and once food starts to sink they will rarely bother to go after it. Only a very few species will forage for food at lower depths.

The advice is, therefore, to offer, at any one time, only as much food as will be eaten in five minutes. Experience alone will show how much food the fish in any particular tank will eat in that time but, as stated earlier, the natural tendency is to give too much.

The owner should not be worried if healthy fish do not seem to be eating large quantities of food. They usually eat small amounts hungrily but take in only the food that they need. The belief that fish are always hungry and need to eat continuously is wrong. Fish know their digestive capabilities better than their owners. The occasional greedy fish will do himself no good by over-eating, but most eat moderately and will suffer no harm even if two or three meals are missed.

Another point to watch when feeding dried food is that when it comes from the container it must be really dry. It is very easy to introduce a little moisture into the package, and this may cause the contents to rot. Served in this form it would be more dangerous to the fish than an equal amount of food rotting at the bottom of the tank.

Healthy stock need both animal and vegetable matter in their diet, and the first-named is usually supplied in the form of live food.

Daphnia   One of the best-known of the live foods is daphnia, or 'water flea'.

In the summer months daphnia are abundant in ponds and shallow pools, especially those that are almost stagnant. They are not difficult to net but there is a danger in acquiring daphnia in this way, for it is easy to introduce into the tank other minute forms of water life that may be dangerous to the stock.

Daphnia

Some water-life shops stock daphnia regularly, while others sell them occasionally. As they should not be fed to the fish daily it is advisable to rely on the shops for supplies.

Daphnia should be given as sparingly as other foods. To empty a can of them into the tank means that large numbers will be ignored for some time and, as living organisms, they will be using some of the oxygen needed by the fish. In proportion to their food value they use considerable amounts of oxygen, and this is important.

When large numbers of fish are kept there may be some advantage in storing daphnia for a few days. This can be done in a shallow water container having a good surface area. Only 2 in. (5 cm) of water is necessary but the container bottom should be covered with a layer of gravel.

Tubifex   Tubifex worms are also popular with fish. They are extremely thin, red in colour, and 1 in to 1½ in. (2·5 cm to 3·75 cm) long. They live in the mud of slow-moving tidal rivers and are regularly on sale in most water-life shops.

Before being given to the fish, the worms should be stood in a container under a slowly dripping tap, the water being changed from time to time. Treated in this way for several hours the worms can be kept alive for some time and, when given to the fish, will be perfectly clean. Again, they should be given in quantities that are quickly eaten.

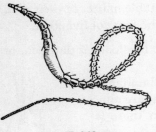

Fish-keepers who cannot buy tubifex worms at a local shop will find that there are firms specialising in the supply of live foods by post, on the basis of a 'once only' order, or in particular quantities at given intervals.

Micro-worm   A live food taken by fish of all sizes is known as micro-worm. These worms are minute, white, and are usually 'cultivated' by the fish-keeper.

Tubifex

Breeding is done in small jars and four or five of these can be started, one every two or three days, so that fresh batches of worms are ready at regular intervals. The culture is inexpensive to buy.

Date-labelled jars for breeding micro-worms.

A spoonful of thin oatmeal porridge is put on the bottom of one of the jars, and a drop of prepared culture is placed in it after the mixture has cooled. This operation is repeated with the remaining jars at the proper intervals.

64

After two days the surface of the porridge will be seen to be 'working' due to the movement of masses of worms, though individually they are too small to be seen with the naked eye.

Once the culture has been working for a few days the question arises as to how to get the worms into the tank without putting in too much of the porridge.

The easiest way is to soak a few match-sticks in cold water. Some of these are placed on the porridge with others laid across to 'bridge' them. Within a few days some micro-worms will have worked their way on to the top layer of match-sticks. As needed, the stick can be lifted with tweezers and rinsed off into the tank.

By using each jar in turn a regular supply of micro-worms is assured but the time must come when the jar is seen to be drying up, and mould may form on the porridge.

A fresh mixture of oatmeal porridge should then be put into a clean jar, and a very little of the old porridge

Collecting micro-worms with match-sticks

used to start the new culture. It is advisable to dispose of the old jar.

White worms   Like micro-worms, white worms are particularly suitable for winter use when other forms of live food may not be readily available.

Again, the worms are bred by the fish-keeper but the culture must be set up three weeks before the first batch is required, so a series of containers may be seeded at intervals of several days.

The worms breed best in an equal mixture of leaf mould and peat, laid to a depth of 2 in. (5 cm) in a suitable container: this needs to be

65

secure along the edges and bottom, or the worms will soon be found where they are not wanted!

The worms need feeding. Oatmeal porridge is suitable but they seem to prefer stale white bread soaked in milk and cut into small cubes.

The food is put into small pockets in the soil and a little of the culture (bought from a water-life store) is placed in each feeding area. The cultures will thrive in the dark at a temperature of 55°F to 65°F (12°C to 18°C); the container may be covered with glass or damp sacking to prevent the soil drying out.

If glass is used the worms will tend to gather on the underside and may be swept off this into the tank. They may also be trapped by laying bread on top of the soil as bait, for the worms will gather under it.

White worms should be rinsed before being given to the fish. They are large enough to be handled with a pair of tweezers and a bunch of them can be doused in a jar of water without any trouble.

Earthworms   The common earthworm is relished by most fish, but they cannot be put into the tank whole. For those who dislike chopping worms into sizes suitable for fish food a shredder may be used.

Mosquito larvae   Mosquito larvae are a useful live food when available, the eggs being collected from ponds, streams or rain-water butts. The eggs resemble clusters of small black grains, and should be kept in a suitable container until they hatch out but they must be given to the fish before they have a chance to develop into adult mosquitoes.

Raw liver   For a change of diet raw liver or beef may be fed to the fish. It is impossible to chop this finely enough so it is scraped off with a fine knife to form a pulp. Other raw meats can be fed in the same way, though pork and other fatty foods should be avoided.

Cyclops   A live food that must be treated with caution is known as 'cyclops'. These are minute shelled creatures of various species and

are sometimes sold at water-life shops, but
not every breed of fish will eat them, and
they are sometimes dangerous to fry or
very young fish.

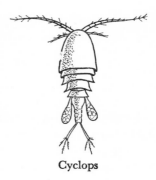

Cyclops

Plant life   It may be noted that some
fish continually nibble at the aquatic
plants: these fish like a high vegetable
content in their diet and if it is lacking
they get it from the plants. Many dried
foods are prepared to a formula and it is
easy enough to select one that has a suitable vegetable content.

Exhibitors and breeders always find feeding to be the greatest
single problem as regards bringing fish into peak condition. Some mix
special dishes of spinach and other vegetables while others find that
certain strained baby foods can be given to the fish in small amounts.

The beginner should not carry things to this length, for feeding in
this way is expensive, wasteful and, except under special circumstances, quite unnecessary. But it does pay to study the likes and dis-
likes of the fish in a particular tank and to adjust their diet
accordingly.

The foods commonly fed to adult fish have now been mentioned, and
some other aspects of fish-keeping may be considered.

7

Maintaining the Tank

SUCCESS with tropical fish-keeping needs patience, common sense, system and cleanliness.

One point often overlooked is that fish must never be handled.

Occasionally a fish leaps while the tank cover is off and flops on to the table or floor. The natural reaction is to grab the fish and put it back in the tank as quickly as possible. Picking up the fish with dry hand or cloth may damage the slimy coating on its body, leading, later, to a disease that can cause its death. Rescue must be prompt, but too much speed can be as bad as too little. The stranded fish should be scooped up in a damp net or with a wet hand.

The hands should be put in the tank only when it is absolutely essential, and the fish must never be disturbed unnecessarily.

When fish are to be netted it will be found an advantage if a large and small net are used simultaneously. A fish can be driven towards the larger net with the smaller, and the net closed with a twist of the wrist when the fish is safely inside. The fish should not be scooped up from beneath. It may be lifted, but some species leap and may jump clear of the tank as the net breaks the surface of the water.

Evaporation will make it necessary to top up the tank with water from time to time. Such water must be of the same temperature as that already in the tank. Cold water may chill the tank far too quickly, and the dangers of extremely hot or boiling water are obvious.

There should be ample warning before such treatment is necessary. This gives plenty of time for the water to be softened as described earlier. Hard water is more common than soft and the softening process is an important factor in maintaining the tank, though no chemical agents may be used.

PLATE 17 · *(Natural size)*

1, 2 & 4. Guppy, males. 3. Guppy, female. 5, 6 & 7. Platy.

(*photos: L. E. Perkins*)

PLATE 18

(*above*)   Swordtails, male and female.
(*below*)   Rosy barbs.

PLATE 19

Tiger and Nigger barbs.

PLATE 20 · (⅔ *natural size*)

1 & 2. Dwarf gourami, male and female.   3. Paradise fish, male (breeding season).   4. Thick-lipped gourami, male.   5. Pearl gourami, male (breeding season).

Pond or river water must never be used for topping up, for such water often contains parasites harmful to tropical fish.

Water will almost certainly retain some hardness. This is not serious as regards fish and plant life, but chalky deposits will gradually build up on the heater.

The first effect will be to make the heater less effective as the deposits have to be warmed through before the heat can be transferred to the water. If the deposits get thick the glass may crack because of the difference in expansion rates of glass and deposits.

When first formed the deposits are soft and can be wiped off easily. According to the hardness of the local water the tube should therefore be lifted and wiped clean periodically.

A heater may go out of action without warning, so it is always as well to have a spare available for emergency use. Note that the tank lighting may not be on the same circuit as the heater. The tank may therefore be illuminated but getting gradually colder because the heater has failed.

A daily test of water temperature with a thermometer is almost essential. In this way the water, while it might get chilled, should never fall to a dangerous temperature level, for it would be extraordinary bad luck for a heater to fail immediately after taking the temperature, thus depriving the tank of heat for a full day.

If possible the temperature should be taken at the same time each day, and similarly the fish should be fed regularly at the same times daily. This is good for the digestion of the fish and it prevents irregular feeding when every member of the family puts food into the tank when the idea occurs to them. The fish soon learn their feeding times if they are regular, and however wary they may be normally, they will come to the top of the tank for food.

Sometimes the tank water takes on a delicate green shade. Under electric lighting this may look attractive but it is a condition that must be cured.

The colour is brought about by minute specks of 'algae' which are microscopic species of underwater plants. To cure the condition one-third of the water is siphoned out and the tank topped up with warm water. The amount of light reaching the tank is then reduced by moving it away from the window if it is sited in such a position, or by putting an electric light bulb of lower wattage in the tank cover.

Algae are a problem for they spread over the glass and grow in the same way as plants. A few can be tolerated, as some fish browse on them happily, but when there are a great number the tank looks dirty and untidy.

There are two main types of algae, 'green' and 'brown'. When they are seen to be forming the cure is simple. Green algae are encouraged by very strong light, brown algae by weak light, so the tank has only to be moved to get more appropriate lighting conditions.

A tank looks its best when illuminated, but if the light is kept on continuously, every day appears (to the fish) to be of the same length. This state of affairs does not exist in nature.

Most fish keep healthier if lighting is reduced during the winter months. This may be done by switching the light on later in the day, or by using a lamp of lower wattage.

At frequent intervals the tank must be cleaned of the waste that drops on to the gravel. This waste is a mixture of uneaten food, rotted leaves and fish excreta, and is removed with a glass siphon tube.

To use the tube the thumb is placed over the top while it is out of the tank. The tube is then put into the tank so that its bottom is about $\frac{1}{2}$ in. (1·25 cm) above the gravel. By lifting the thumb, pressure forces water and some waste matter into the tube. The latter is closed by again placing the thumb over the top and it may then be lifted out of the tank and emptied.

The glass siphon tube is useful because it can be directed at plants, over crevices in rock-work, and so on, to make cleaning fairly easy. It does take a certain amount of water out of the tank with the waste. which means that the tank may need topping up at frequent intervals,

Fish that are obviously unwell must undergo a period in an isolation tank. Certain equipment will be used for netting and maintaining sick fish, and the possibility of introducing bacteria into the tank by means of this should not be overlooked.

These remarks apply particularly to nets. A separate net should always be kept for handling sick fish and it should be sterilised by boiling after use.

Much of the beauty of an aquarium is due to the plants. Nearly all aquatic plants spread quickly during the summer, and the plan for the underwater garden is lost by excessive development.

A tank that is too densely planted means that the fish are seen only occasionally as they are usually lurking behind plant growth, and the density of the leaves may drastically reduce the amount of essential light reaching the tank.

Plants should be thinned out in late autumn. Some will naturally die back at that time and during the winter, but if they are not thinned there will be excessive growth during the following spring. It is preferable to do any rearranging of the plants at the start of the winter season (even though, in an aquarium, this is a somewhat artificial season) than it is in the spring when plants are beginning to make new growth.

Not all plants do equally well in a tank and they may be as puzzling to the fish-keeper as trees and shrubs to the keen gardener. Given two tanks side by side, apparently identical in all respects, it will be found that in one a particular species will thrive and in the other it will simply die off. This is one of the unaccountable quirks of aquarium-keeping and must be accepted as such.

However carefully the dip tube or siphon is used, rock-work in the tank tends to become greasy. Vigorous scrubbing of the stone, followed by boiling it, will help to keep the water crystal clear.

Limestone, gypsum and other stones with a high lime content should never be used in the tank, because the water hardens as the lime gradually dissolves. Sandstone is available in several different colours and is very good for most aquarium rock-work.

A condition usually described as 'black sand' sometimes develops in a tank and is brought about by insufficient care in clearing away waste material.

Outwardly the gravel appears in reasonable condition but an occasional bubble is to be seen coming out of the compost and floating up to the surface. This is a bubble of gas that has been trapped beneath the gravel.

If the surface is raked with the end of a dip tube, the gravel will be found black in colour and if a little is taken up in the tube and examined it will be found to have a foul, penetrating smell.

The only possible remedy is to clear out all the gravel and put in fresh compost.

This is a major job that cannot be done without transferring the fish and plants to another tank capable of accommodating them with safety. Before the original tank can be used again it will have to be sterilised and then treated as if it were being set up for the first time.

A bad attack of black sand will be more effective than a dozen pages of print in emphasising the need to prevent the bottom of the tank from getting foul.

Dirt and dust sometimes gather on the surface of the water. This can be floated off with the help of a piece of newspaper or polythene sheet. Algae and grease on the sides of the tank can be scraped off (using a razor blade fixed to a long, thin stick) and the resultant rubbish taken out of the tank with a dip tube.

Razor blade on stick for cleaning sides of glass

Some fish-keepers periodically treat the tank with a pinch of Epsom salts, or add a spoonful to the water if some of the fish are seen to be trailing a long stream of excreta. This latter is a sign of constipation and may affect only one or two of the fish in the tank. It is therefore preferable to treat the individual fish in a separate tank on the lines laid down in Chapter 10 rather than to periodically dose all the inhabitants of a tank.

Although fish can withstand a temperature variation within a range of 10°F (6°C), such a change must take place only gradually. At all costs a sudden drop in temperature must be avoided, as this may result in sickness in the tank.

Perfect fish health depends on adequate and suitable diet. As already pointed out, although the fish may show decided preferences for certain foods, their diet must be varied.

One method that fish-keepers have found useful when giving dried food is to mix it to a crumbly paste with a little Bemax, Marmite, or other concentrated food. As a 'conditioner', cod liver oil or something similar is also used in the same way. Boosted diets of this type should be given only infrequently.

A milky clouding of the water may occur from time to time, the condition being described as 'milky water'. This is caused by over-feeding with dried foods, more especially those with a high starch content.

The remedy is obvious. The amount of food given at any time must be cut down and more live food introduced into the diet. A little water can be siphoned off daily and the tank topped up with fresh, until the water again becomes quite clear.

The problem of feeding the fish over a holiday period sometimes puzzles the beginner.

The first thing to remember is that adult fish of small breeds can go without food for nearly three weeks without suffering serious harm. For larger breeds an even longer period is possible.

With an ordinary week-end away from home there is no real problem. A normal feed is given at the usual time before departure and another on return. The natural tendency to make these feeds large ones must be resisted.

If the holiday is to last five days or more the bulb in the tank hood should be replaced with one of lower wattage. This will not be necessary, however, if the lighting is controlled by a time switch.

Over a longer holiday period it may be possible to get an experienced friend to feed the fish daily. A non-experienced friend could be given the same job (1) if all meals were packaged and (2) if it were made clear that only one meal a day should be given and that if he cannot deal with the fish on any day they must miss that meal and not be given double rations later. Packaging of dried foods is easy enough, and live foods can be done up in small plastic bags or containers.

Even with instructions as clear as this it must be anticipated that, on return from a long holiday, the tank will need to be tidied up and put into good trim again. There is no need, however, for the fish-keeper to feel that his being away has put the health of his stock in danger.

8

Breeding Tropical Fish

ANY fish-keeper with a mature male and female guppy in a community tank will sooner or later be a fish 'breeder'. For reasons to be explained, he may never see the young, but they will have been born.

Fish breeding can be 'accidental' or 'controlled'.

Controlled breeding has one of two ends in view. Firstly, it may be to increase the number of fish owned at little expense to the owner, and secondly it may be intended for improving the breed as regards certain desirable characteristics.

This second type of fish breeding is highly scientific and beyond the scope of the beginner. Yet nobody can pass on to specialised fish breeding until experience has been gained in the simpler aspects.

This chapter describes only the breeding of fish to increase their number, not to improve the strain. General aspects of fish breeding will first be considered, and this will be followed by remarks on the breeding habits and needs of some of the more common species. The emphasis, however, is on controlled breeding, not on the casual mating of a pair in the community tank.

When producing young, fish can be divided into two main classes.

Firstly, there are 'live-bearers'. These produce their young from the body of the mother as fully formed, free-swimming fish. The fry are able to take certain foods (for example, micro-worms) from birth, and they are extremely active.

When the fry is born it immediately darts towards the nearest plant, rock-work or other shelter. Adult fish (including the parents) may show marked cannibalistic tendencies towards the fry, and the quick dart to safety is nature's defence mechanism. In a community tank many fry will fall victim to adult fish, but others will keep well hidden until they have grown to a safer size.

75

The second method of producing young is by egg-laying. During the hatching period the developing fish absorb the contents of their egg, but once free-swimming fish they require ordinary diets to grow to maturity.

Unless precautions are taken, the chances of eggs surviving in a community tank are few.

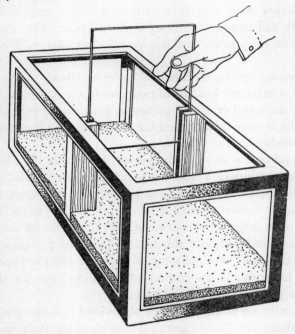

Removable glass partition for conditioning parents before mating

Although both kinds of fish can be bred under controlled conditions the most successful results, at the start, will probably be with the live-bearers. Early experiments in breeding should therefore be taken with a pair of guppies.

It is advisable to breed the fish during the spring and summer months only. The parents-to-be need careful selection, and they must be both mature and in perfect health.

It is usual to condition the parents before mating by separating them, often in a tank with a removable glass partition between the sexes so that the fish can see, but not come into contact with each other. The amount of live food given is stepped up quite sharply and the dried food cut down by a corresponding amount.

The breeding tank can be quite shallow and does not need setting up with rock-work, but it will be an advantage if the heat of the water can be readily adjusted.

With the live-bearers water temperature has a big effect on the time between mating and birth of the fry. At a constant water temperature of 75°F (24°C) live-bearers will produce their young in about half the time necessary if the temperature is held at 68°F (20°C) in general, the shorter the period before birth the stronger the fry will be, so the water should be held at a constant temperature of 75°F (24°C).

Several births result from one fertilisation of the female, the fry being born at intervals over a number of days. Mating will take place when the partition between the sexes is removed.

The cannibalistic tendencies of some parents have already been mentioned. These can be defeated by the use of a breeding trap, or by removal of the male once the female has been fertilised. Nothing should be done, however, that will frighten the female.

In the case of egg-laying breeds there are slight differences as regards the actual breeding and treatment.

Plants are very important in breeding tanks for egg-layers. Unless particularly required by the breed, aquarium gravel is not laid, and the plants are anchored into place with lead sinkers.

The adults are brought into breeding condition by separation and feeding up on live foods. When the time is considered ripe for mating the male is put in with the female overnight.

Spawning usually takes place in the early morning. The male chases the female, releasing the fertilising fluid as she releases her eggs. In some cases the eggs are sticky, in others non-adhesive. The non-sticky eggs will fall to the bottom of the tank, and the others will stick to the plants, glass or gravel.

The male stops chasing the female once all his fertilising fluid has been ejected and the female has laid her eggs; the latter are fertilised by contact with the fluid. Normally, immediately spawning is over, both adults should be netted and returned to the main tank. If this is not done the fish may start to eat the eggs.

Fry of fish with egg-sac

The eggs must remain undisturbed until they hatch. When this happens the fry will be almost transparent and will have a sac containing food under their bodies, but the egg-sac will gradually disappear and the fry then become free-swimming fish.

The time between egg-laying and hatching will vary from approximately two to seven days according to breed, water temperature, etc. Hatching is followed by an inactive period while the food-sac is absorbed. During this period no food should be put into the tank. The fry of egg-layers can be fed (first on infusoria then on micro-worms) only when they are free-swimming.

With an idea of the basic requirements of live-bearers and egg-layers some mention might be made of parental habits.

Cannibalism towards the young is most common with live-bearing and toothed species, and with young parents.

Some species are aggressive in defence of their breeding areas and in caring for the young, though such problems cause no trouble in proper breeding tanks.

The care of the fry is sometimes the responsibility of both parents or only one, or, in a few cases, neither.

In the former case each parent may guard the young in turn or make alternative arrangements for their safety. For example, some breeds transfer the fry to small depressions in the gravel and confine them strictly to certain limits. This guardianship will be kept up until a new brood is due, when the young fish will be chased away. In a breeding tank the young fish will have been removed before this latter stage is reached.

When the care of the young falls on one parent the female is usually responsible, though with some breeds the roles are reversed.

In cases where the female is responsible for the fry the male should be removed from the tank immediately after spawning. If not, the female may attack him, sometimes most viciously, and as the male loses his natural aggressiveness at this time he may be badly injured. The maternal instinct disappears when the female is ready for a fresh spawning, and she will then turn on the young fish.

The reverse occurs when it is the male that guards the fry.

The methods of guarding the young are many. They include vicious attacks on possible intruders and hiding the fry in the rock-work or in dense plant growth, round which a constant patrol is kept. With certain breeds the young are taken into the mouths of the parents when danger threatens. The fry are rarely damaged by this treatment and even less rarely is one accidentally killed. Fish showing this type of family care are known as mouth-breeders.

There are also the bubble-nest breeds. With these the males make a nest by blowing bubbles on to the top of the tank to form a fragile nest that has constantly to be kept in repair. The eggs are laid direct into the nest and if any fall out they are carefully replaced by the male. Young fish, also, are replaced when they get out, but the time comes when the fry are too active to be restrained. The adult male must then be removed as he will go frantic trying to keep the fry under control, and he may go on a killing spree.

Notes now follow on the breeding characteristics of some of the more popular tropical breeds.

Angel fish   One of the difficulties here is that it is not easy to distinguish the sex of the adults. The best solution for the beginner is to keep a number of adults in a tank confined to angel fish and let nature take its course.

Eggs are laid on a smooth surface and many experts recommend a piece of slate (with one edge slightly raised) in the bottom of the tank. Both parents assist in fanning the eggs, and spend a considerable amount of time in moving newly hatched fry from one place to another within the tank.

Bloodfins   These breed only in soft water and the tank must be well planted as they prefer to mate in dense foliage. The eggs are adhesive.

With bloodfins the tank *must* be covered as the male, in particular, is an expert jumper and can well leap out of the tank.

Both parents must be removed immediately after spawning, as they are avid egg-eaters.

Dwarf gourami   An interesting species as it is a bubble-nest breeder but unusual in that the female also helps to build the nest.

A small rock-work cave is needed in the tank, for courtship is a very rough business and if not ready for the spawning the female may be severely mauled. A hiding place can therefore be useful.

The male wraps his body round the female and they roll round each other briefly, releasing a few eggs. The mating process is repeated several times until all the eggs are laid, when the female retreats to her hiding place.

Guppy   This is a very prolific breeder and from one act of fertilisation young will be born over a period of many months. Mating may occur at a very early age, but should be prevented, if possible, until the fish are at least six months old. This is a live-bearing breed.

Cannibalism is rampant but may be prevented (or at least mini-mised) by feeding heavily with live food during the conditioning period.

Mollies   One of the features of the courtship is the display of fins by the male. This is a live-bearing breed and the parents must be well conditioned on live foods prior to mating.

The tank must be planted densely but the normal temperature is adequate. It is advisable to keep the pair in a separate tank, and some experts recommend that a small pinch of salt should be put into the water. The male should be removed before the first of the young is born, so as to leave the female undisturbed in a tank with which she is familiar.

Pearl danio With this species it is the female that makes the first advances and, after a while, the male takes up the chase and mating follows. The resulting eggs are non-adhesive.

Shallow water is necessary and the parents must be removed immediately after spawning. It is customary to 'mass spawn' with this breed, using two males to one female or three males to two females, but for this a fairly long tank is needed, otherwise the fish may damage themselves against the glass.

Platy A live-bearer needing only the normal treatment given to such varieties. The platy will mate quite well with other live-bearer breeds.

Rosy barb Prefers a high temperature (approximately 80°F or 27°C) for spawning and hatching. It is a variety with which mass spawning is often practised, two females being put in the tank in the morning and three males at night. All fish must be ready for spawning, otherwise those who do not take part eat the eggs that are laid. The tank must be reasonably densely planted, as the eggs are laid as the fish drive through the plants. Eggs are adhesive and most stick to the leaves.

Sharks The eggs are scattered haphazardly (being fertilised as they are laid) and they sink to the bottom of the tank. Mating is started by the female driving the male, but the roles are soon reversed. Some varieties are not easy to mate successfully.

Siamese fighter Mating should not be allowed until the fish are a year old. Courtship is a rough business and although the female is sufficiently alert to avoid trouble, slight misjudgment could mean her death. A rock-work hiding place should be provided and the female should be left in the breeding tank for some days before the male is introduced.

This is an egg-laying, bubble-nesting breed, with the male responsible for the building of the nest.

When laid, all the eggs fall to the bottom of the tank but are put in the nest by both parents. The female should be removed when spawning (usually complete in two to three hours) has obviously finished.

The care shown by the male is interesting. When not repairing the nest or rescuing the fry he hovers below the nest, fanning it and the eggs with his fins. Nevertheless this does not prevent him attacking and killing the fry when they get too active for his liking.

Swordtail   A prolific live-bearer but if the fish are to do well they must be brought on without a check, and over-crowding avoided. It is therefore necessary to divide the fry among a number of tanks as they grow.

Both parents may prove to be cannibals but, again, heavy feeding with live food before mating may help to minimise trouble.

White cloud mountain minnow   Breeding can be practised from the age of six months onwards, but the stock must be well conditioned on live food.

The species is notorious for egg-eating and it is difficult to judge when the parents should be removed as egg-laying may continue for twenty-four hours.

The simplest way to defeat egg-eating is to use a shallow tank and to cover the base with a fair matting of aquatic plants, anchored with lead sinkers. Mountain minnow eggs are not sticky and fall through the leaves to the base where the parents find difficulty in getting at them. This is a species for which a breeding trap can be used to advantage.

9

Feeding the Fry

When one considers the minute size of the fry when they first become free-swimming, it is not surprising that they cannot take food suitable for adult fish.

They must be fed on 'infusoria' for the first few days of life or until they show signs of being able to cope with a more substantial diet. The general rules must be that meals should be given more frequently than for adults (though over-feeding must be avoided) and the change from baby food to adult diet must be smooth and progressive.

The description 'infusoria' covers a wide range of tiny aquatic creatures. Individually they are too small to be seen with the naked eye, but in great numbers they appear as a cloudy mass that obviously has some form of life in it.

Infusoria are bred from such things as hay and lettuce leaves. For this purpose some large glass jars will be needed.

Lettuce leaves are the easiest things from which to raise infusoria. A jar of aquarium water (preferably from a tank established some months) is taken and lettuce leaves are bruised and put into this. The jar is stored in a dark place at a temperature of from 55°F to 65°F (12°C to 18°C) and in about four days the jar will be swarming with infusoria.

To use hay for breeding infusoria two handfuls are boiled and the dark brown liquid strained off. An equal amount of mature aquarium water is added, plus a small handful of garden sub-soil.

Stored in the dark at the temperature suggested earlier, this will develop a good crop of infusoria, though it is slower to develop than the lettuce culture.

One objection to breeding infusoria is that after a time it develops a foul, penetrating smell. If sufficient jars are started at intervals of three days, for example, it is possible to have ample food supplies yet get rid of jars as soon as the smell is objectionable.

The fry of egg-layers take infusoria as soon as they are free swimming. The first jar is therefore started as soon as male and female are put together. Live-bearer fry also take infusoria as soon as they are born, but it is more difficult to estimate when the culture should be started so as to have the infusoria ready for the fry.

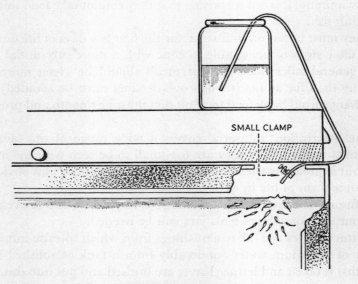

SMALL CLAMP

Drip feeding infusoria

If live-bearers and egg-layers are being bred at the same time there should be no problem as one jar will produce a considerable quantity of this minute live food. Two tablespoons of infusoria liquid make an adequate meal for about fifty fry.

'Drip feeding' is often used to get the infusoria into the tank.

The infusoria are put through a very fine mesh net into clean water at tank temperature. The container is stood on the aquarium hood so that it keeps warm, and an extremely fine siphon tube is put between this and the tank. With a small clamp or spring clip the tube

PLATE 21 · (½ *natural size*)

1. Jack Dempsey.   2. Jewel cichlid.   3. Striped cichlid.

(*photo: L. E. Perkins*)

PLATE 22
Pompadour fish.

PLATE 23
Sleeper fish.

PLATE 24 · (⅓ *natural size*)

1. Brown acara.   2. Angel fish.   3. Pompadour fish.

is closed down even more, so that only a minute trickle of infusoria is fed continuously into the tank of fry. The weight of the hood helps to restrict the flow of infusoria through the pipe, but the main control is exercised by the clamp.

Brine shrimp eggs can be bought for hatching and the shrimps fed to live-bearer fry as soon as they are born, and to egg-layers when they take an active interest in food. The eggs remain fertile however long they are stored. They will take from twenty-four to forty-eight hours to hatch. A few eggs should be placed in a gallon of water to which four tablespoons of sea salt have been added. The normal aquarium temperature of 70°F to 72°F (21°C to 22°C) will provide sufficient warmth for hatching.

Brine shrimp

Proprietary foods in tubes are available, sold separately for live-bearer and egg-laying fry. They are in liquid or semi-liquid form and are clean and easy to feed to the fry. They are particularly valuable when a number of tanks for fry are being maintained, and are also economical as the food is not exposed to the air and keeps fresh longer than most home-made diets.

An excellent food for very young fish (including newly hatched egg-layers) is an egg yolk liquid.

For this, an egg is boiled for fifteen minutes so that it is exceptionally hard. The yolk is then rubbed through a very fine meshed sieve into a cup of water to make a thin, yellow mixture. Any solid matter getting into the liquid must be strained off, and the watery feed can be given twice a day.

Making diets in this way is wasteful when the actual quantity of food produced is considered because, usually, after one day the balance must be thrown away before it goes bad. Some wastage can be eliminated by freezing the surplus, but once thawed out it cannot be re-frozen.

Freezing does mean that, with a diet like egg yolk liquid, twice the number of normal feeds may be obtained. In America, frozen fish foods are sold extensively, and the stock does not appear to come to any harm by being fed on them.

Young fish share the diet taste of their elders and when large enough they appreciate a meal of fish eggs or roe. These must be of a size suitable for the fish and, as always, not too many may be given at one time.

Various prepared fish pastes (crab, salmon, etc.) can be given when the fish are taking fairly substantial meals. The paste needs to be crumbled finely and, if not consumed quickly, must be removed from the tank. An alternative method of feeding such paste is as a watery mixture which can be drip fed in the way described above.

Micro-worms are an excellent live food for young fish.

The very fine dust mixed with even the most carefully packed dried food is also an excellent diet for young fish. The dust must be carefully sieved so that only the smallest grains are fed.

As the fish develop it will be found that they grow more steadily if the numbers in the tank are thinned out. This will prevent any battle for the available food, for even if supplies are adequate some of the weaker fish will be harried at meal times by their more aggressive brothers and sisters.

10

Ailments of Tropical Fish

TROPICAL fish kept in a tank that is properly cared for should remain healthy. Even so, it can hardly be expected that a fish will live out the whole of its life without occasionally showing signs of being off colour, and this state may be brought about by conditions that are outside the fish-keeper's control.

Usually the trouble will be only a minor one, and easily cleared up by a suitable treatment. Many fish may be suffering from a similar minor complaint at the one time, and all will be quite easily cured. Much less frequently the trouble will be more serious, and a number of fish will die, suggesting that some form of infectious disease has got into the tank.

A fish that is sick can be recognised by its listlessness, lack of colour, and drooping fins; with those breeds that hold the dorsal fin erect it is usually this fin that is the first to droop. There may be symptoms that suggest what is causing the sickness, and this means that the probable remedy is also indicated.

When the trouble is more serious, and a large number of deaths are occurring, the best thing to do is to get expert advice. The body of the fish can be sent for a post-mortem examination. It is wrapped wet in damp greaseproof paper, then in a dry cloth, and finally in dry greaseproof paper, and is sent to a specialist who will give a report on it. The name of a specialist can be chosen from the advertisement pages of one of the magazines devoted to fish-keeping. The cost of this service is only a few shillings, and it may save the lives of many other fish in the tank by drawing attention to the real cause of the trouble.

One of the most common minor complaints is constipation. This does not necessarily make the fish less active, but it trails a thread of excreta behind it.

To some extent this trouble can be kept in check by putting a pinch of Epsom salts in the tank at the beginning of each month. If the trouble continues, the constipated fish may be put into a separate tank (preferably with water from the main tank) in which a table-spoon of the salts has been mixed to every gallon of water in the treatment tank. The fish can be left in this tank for twenty-four hours, and then be returned to the main tank, but if the trouble is not cleared up by one treatment, it may be repeated on alternate days. The depth of water in the treatment tank can be quite shallow, and neither plants nor gravel are required. It may be of some help if the temperature is raised to a few degrees above that of the main tank.

Digestive troubles, sometimes caused by over-eating, may be cured by the same treatment. With these, the fish is languid and the stomach is usually seen to be slightly swollen.

It may be noted at this point that for many of the ailments mentioned in this chapter specially packaged medicines are sold by the water-life shops. These remedies can be very effective if they are handled in the way recommended by the makers.

Different fish breeds react differently to change of water temperature, and some can suffer a steady drop of temperature (such as might happen during a power cut) much more happily than others. A sudden drop in temperature is dangerous to all breeds, however, and although any particular breed may be hardy, there is a temperature below which trouble will occur. What happens, in fact, is that the fish catches a chill.

Signs of a chill are the dejected attitude of the fish and apparent difficulty in swimming. If all the fish are affected they may be treated in their own tank, but if only a few have taken a chill, they should be transferred to a separate, shallow tank. The water temperature is then raised by some 4°F to 5°F (2°C) each hour until it reaches almost 90°F (32°C), and is kept at that figure for twenty-four hours. Temperature is then reduced by not more than 5°F (2°C) every day until the water is at the normal tank temperature.

Sometimes a fish is seen to be unduly excited, darting around the tank, coming up often to the surface, and sometimes flopping helplessly on to its side. This is almost invariably a sign of acute oxygen distress. An immediate cure can usually be made by emptying half of the water out of the tank and replacing it with an equal amount of water at the same temperature. This is a cure but not a remedy. The next step must be to see what was causing the lack of oxygen, and to put those conditions right. Almost certainly the water will have been poisoned by decayed food or something similar.

Tropical fish sometimes suffer from cuts that result from brushing against sharp-edged aquarium ornaments or something similar. This is a normal hazard of life for an aquarium fish, and unless the wound

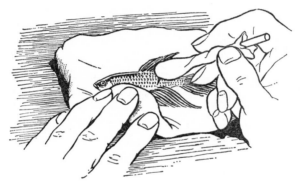

Disinfecting the fish with swab

is so severe that it causes trouble to the fish when swimming, a wound is not really important. However, there is always the point that a cut is an open gateway for infection, so it is just as well to disinfect the wound.

Popular disinfectants are mercurochrome, iodine and acriflavine, the first-named being the one that is favoured by most fish-keepers. It is usually sold as a 2 per cent solution, but when it is used as a bath rather than as a swab it must be diluted with nine parts of water.

The fish to be treated must be netted and placed on a large pad of really wet cloth, and the affected area swabbed with a piece of soft lint wrapped round an orange stick, or with a larger pad held in a pair of tweezers. Obviously, the fish must be returned to its tank as soon as possible but under no circumstances should the fish be handled with dry fingers. The advice that is often given to use cotton wool for the swabbing is not really sound, as the material is too easily caught up in the wound.

The treated fish should be kept under observation for a couple of days, and, if necessary the treatment repeated. Too strong a disinfectant must not be used otherwise a scar will develop on the body of the fish, and similarly, a disinfecting treatment must not be repeated at too frequent intervals.

Cotton-wool fungus

A fish that has been damaged, or is in poor health may be attacked by a fungus disease that is often called 'cotton-wool fungus'.

In the early stages the white threads of the fungus appear, sparsely, on the body, but this soon develops into a fairly dense mat. The fins will then start to contract, and although the fish is hardly likely to die as a result of the trouble, it will be a very sorry looking specimen indeed. Other fish in the tank will also be contaminated and develop the fungus. If the fungus is noticed early enough, the cure is quite simple. The sick fish should (as always) be transferred to a separate tank, and it will be necessary to swab the fungus or bathe the fish.

Swabbing can be done with mercurochrome or diluted iodine in the way described above. Bathing for a recommended period in one of the proprietary medicines will usually cure the most stubborn case of fungus, and it is also possible to use a bath made of diluted mercurochrome, etc. For the beginner it is always better to use a proprietary medicine rather than a diluted disinfectant, for any mistake with the latter can lead to severe damage to the fish, or even its death. With ready mixed medicines that need diluting, it is essential that it be diluted in the quantities quoted by the manufacturer.

Whatever the ailment from which the fish is suffering, the symptoms often start in much the same way, which may cause some doubt as to the proper treatment. The loss of colour, and then general droopiness, has already been mentioned. Quite often the scales of the fish seem to stand away from its body. This in itself is not serious, but it can be the early warning signs of swim bladder trouble or dropsy.

Swim bladder trouble may develop as the result of a chill. The fish seems to have difficulty in swimming, moves about at an awkward angle very different from the normal swimming attitude of its breed, and keeps to the bottom of the tank, seeming to lack buoyancy. The condition cannot be mistaken for ordinary oxygen distress. Eventually, unable to swim or get food, the fish will die.

Fortunately the trouble takes a long time to develop and the fish can usually be saved if action is taken early. The fish should be transferred to a separate tank and the temperature raised some 10°F (6°C) above the normal tank temperature. After prolonged heat tank treatment the fish will normally perk up again.

Dropsy is a different matter, and many experienced fish-keepers are convinced that there is no real cure for this disease, though there are certain medicines that can be mixed in with the food that may help in the early stages. Prompt isolation of the fish is necessary.

The disease attacks the kidneys and liver of the fish, and the stomach gets badly bloated. The progress of the disease is swift, and the fish probably suffers severely. (It is a mistake to think that fish cannot feel pain.) If a heated tank treatment or suitable medicine does not bring about a rapid change for the better in the fish the kindest thing to do is to kill it.

Two of the ailments most feared by fish-keepers are 'white spot' and 'velvet spot', for the first named can spread rapidly to infect all the fish in a tank and the death rate may be high. Velvet spot acts more slowly but can also be fatal.

The first-named disease is sometimes called 'ich,' an abbreviation of its Latin name, *Ichthyophthirius multifiliis*.

The early symptoms are similar to those in all forms of parasite disease. The fish scrapes itself against the rock-work or tank sides or

shakes its fins vigorously, trying to free itself of the parasites. Later, small white irregular dots appear on the body of the fish, these rapidly increasing in number. The fish loses its appetite, becomes less active and then dies, the whole process taking only a relatively short time.

The sequence of the attack is as follows.

A young parasite attaches itself to the fish, feeding on the body tissue around it, and, at the same time, re-

White spot

leasing certain poisons into that tissue. When fully grown it leaves the body of the fish, sinks to the bottom of the tank, forms a ball (called a cyst) inside an outer covering of slime and, by a process of cell division, multiplies itself several hundred times within the course of less than one day. The young emerge, bore into the body of any available fish, and raise another 'white spot' to start the whole life cycle again.

It will be seen that even if the tank contained only one parasite to begin with, it would not take long for the whole tank to be infected with them.

The object of a white spot treatment is to destroy the cysts before the young parasites can emerge, and only then to kill the adults already in the bodies of the fish.

One simple way of disposing of the cysts and free-swimming parasites is to remove all the fish to a separate tank for a period of ten days. With no hosts to batten on, the young parasites will die off.

This means that the parasites in the body of the fish are still alive and ready to start new life cycles in the new tank.

Methylene blue is highly regarded as a white spot cure, and, in fact, is regarded by aquarists as a universal cure-all.

A 5 per cent aqueous solution of methylene blue is poured into an unplanted tank holding the sick fish, a sufficient quantity being used to stain the water a deep blue. The fish can be left in the tank for a minimum of ten days, by which time the white spots should have disappeared, and the fish can be returned to their ordinary tank with safety.

As an alternative to the methylene blue, a mercurochrome bath may be used. This can be a 2 per cent solution diluted with nine parts of water, the fish being given a fifteen minute bath daily for seven days. The water in the tank in which the fish are kept when not in the disinfectant bath should have the water temperature raised by some 10°F (6°C) above the normal tank temperature.

Velvet spot

When using a tank for quarantine and 'hospital' purposes it is essential that it be thoroughly cleaned out and disinfected before it is again taken into normal use. This is particularly important in the case of parasitic diseases.

Velvet spot, as mentioned above, is much slower in its action than white spot.

This condition can be recognised by small yellowish-brown specks on the skin, almost like grains of sand. The trouble is caused by a tiny parasite that attaches itself to the outside of the fish and, in the early stages of attack, does not appear to worry it. A rather stronger methylene blue bath than was used for white spot will make a suitable bath for curing velvet spot. Acriflavine and aureomycin are

93

other suitable remedies, but are much more drastic than methylene blue, and need to be used with some care, otherwise the remedy may be worse than the disease.

There are very many forms of parasite, attacking the fish in different ways and all having a weakening effect on the fish. Parasite attack of one form or another is to be suspected whenever a fish is seen to be continually scraping itself against rocks or the glass panels of the tank.

One of the effects of parasite attack is that the fish will be weakened and unable to withstand other forms of disease. One of the parasites

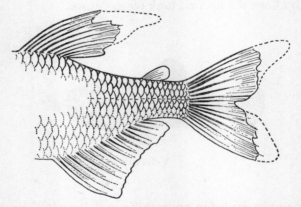

Fin and tail rot. (Dotted lines indicate original extent of fins.)

that is rather dangerous in itself is the gill fluke, which as its name suggests, attaches itself to the gills of its host. Yet gill flukes, like all other parasites, can be destroyed by disinfectant baths.

Another form of fungal disease can result in fin and tail rot. The signs of this are very obvious, the membrane of the fins shrinking, breaking away, and gradually disintegrating. Again, the affected fish will become a very sorry looking specimen. The fin rot should therefore be corrected as soon as possible. The disinfectants and antibiotics previously mentioned will be effective.

The manufacturers of pet foods produce a wide range of scientifically prepared 'tonics', designed to keep the fish as healthy as possible. Experience has proved that these can be quite effective, and their use can be recommended.

From the length of this chapter it might be thought that fish ailments and diseases are a constant worry to the keeper of tropical fish. This is far from being the case. If normal care is taken, tropical fish will be found to be very hardy little creatures but it is as well to know what to do on the rare occasions when trouble does develop.

Appendix

The scientific names of some popular tropical fish

SCIENTIFIC NAME	POPULAR NAME
Aequidens portalegrensis	Brown acara or green acara
Aphyocharax rubropinnis	Bloodfin
Aphyosemion australe	Lyre-tail
Barbus everetti	Clown barb
Barbus pentazona	Five-banded barb
Barbus ticto	Two-spot barb
Betta splendens	Siamese fighter
Brachydanio albolineatus	Pearl danio
Brachydanio nigrofasciatus	Spotted danio
Brachydanio rerio	Zebra fish
Brachygobius numus	Bumble bee
Capoeta tetrazona	Tiger barb
Cheirodon alexrodi	Cardinal tetra
Chilodus punctatus	Headstander
Cichlasoma biocellatum	Jack Dempsey
Cichlasoma meeki	Firemouth cichlid
Cichlasoma severum	Striped cichlid
Colisa labiosa	Thick-lipped gourami
Colisa lalia	Dwarf gourami
Copeina arnoldi	Splashing tetra
Corydoras aenus	Bronze catfish
Corydoras julii	Leopard catfish
Corydoras apleatus	Spotted catfish, or peppered catfish
Cynolebias bellottii	Argentine pearl
Danio malabaricus	Giant danio
Dormator maculatus	Sleeper fish
Epiplatys chaperi	Red-throated panchax
Esomus danricus	Flying barb
Gasteropelecus sternicla	Silver hatchet
Gymnocorymbus ternetzi	Black widow
Gyrinocheillus aymonieri	Sucking loach

97

SCIENTIFIC NAME	POPULAR NAME
Haplorchromis multicolor	Egyptian mouth-breeder
Helostoma temmincki	Kissing gourami
Hemichromis bimaculatus	Jewel cichlid
Hemigrammus ocellifer	Beacon fish
Hemigrammus unilineatus	Feather fin
Hyphessobrycon flammeus	Flame fish
Hyphessobrycon gracilis	Glowlight tetra
Hyphessobrycon heterorhabdus	Belgian flag tetra
Hyphessobrycon innesi	Neon tetra
Hyphessobrycon pulchripinnis	Lemon tetra
Hyphessobrycon rosaceus	Rosy tetra, or black flag
Hyphessobrycon scholzei	Blackline tetra
Jordanell floridae	American flag fish
Labeo bicolor	Red-tailed black shark
Lebistes reticulatus	Guppy, or millions fish
Macropodus opercularis	Paradise fish
Melanotaenia macculochi	Australian rainbow
Moenkhausia pittieri	Diamond tetra
Mollienisia latipinna	Sailfin molly
Mollienisia schwarz	Black molly
Mollienisia sphenops	Liberty molly
Nannobrycon eques	One-striped pencil fish, or red-tailed pencil fish
Nannostomus trifasciatus	Three-striped pencil fish
Nematobrycon palmeri	Emperor tetra
Otocinclus affinis	Otocinclus catfish
Panchax lineatus	Lined panchax
Pelmatochromis kribensis	Dwarf rainbow cichlid
Plecostomus plecostomus	Sucking catfish
Pristella riddlei	X-ray fish
Pterophyllum eimekei	Angel fish
Pterophyllum scalare	Angel fish
Puntius conchonius	Rosy barb
Puntius nigrofasciatus	Nigger barb
Puntius oligolepis	Checkered barb
Puntius titteya	Cherry barb
Rasbora heteromorpha	Harlequin fish

SCIENTIFIC NAME	POPULAR NAME
Rivulus urophthalmus	Red rivulus
Symphysodon discus	Pompadour fish
Tanichthys albonubes	White cloud mountain minnow
Trichogaster leeri	Pearl gourami, or lace gourami
Trichogaster trichopterus	Blue gourami
Xiphophorus helleri	Swordtail
Xiphophorus maculatus	Platy

Bibliography

BOOKS

THE following is a very brief list of books likely to be useful to readers wishing to make a study of particular breeds, or other aspects of tropical fish-keeping.

Anon *Tropical Aquarium for Beginners* (Ditchfield British Books, Leyland, Lancs.)

Anon *Tropical Fish Keeping* (Ditchfield British Books, Leyland, Lancs.)

Axelrod, H. R. *Breeding Aquarium Fishes* (T.F.H. Publications, London)

Axelrod, H. R. and Vorderwinkler, W. *Encyclopedia of Tropical Fishes* (Ward Lock, London)

Cooper, Allan *Fishes of the World* (Paul Hamlyn, London)

Dutta, Reginald *Manual for Fish Tank Owners* (Pelham Books, London)

Elwin, M. G. *Tropical Fishes* (Iliffe Books, London)

Emmens, C. W. *How to Keep and Feed Tropical Fish* (T.F.H. Publications, London)

Ervin, Mabel *Enjoy Your Mollies* (Pet Library, London)

Frey, Hans *Illustrated Dictionary of Tropical Fishes* (T.F.H. Publications, London)

Friswold, Carroll *Enjoy Your Guppies* (Pet Library, London)

Friswold, Carroll *Enjoy Your Fancy Guppies* (Pet Library, London)

Ghadially, F. N. *Advanced Aquarist* (Pet Library, London)

Ghadially, F. N. *Fighting Fish of Siam* (Aquarist & Pondkeeper, Brentford, Middlesex)

Haas, Richard *Enjoy Breeding Egg-layers* (Pet Library, London)

Haas, Richard *Enjoy Breeding Live-bearers* (Pet Library, London)

Hervey, G. F. and Hems, J. *Freshwater Tropical Aquarium Fishes* (Spring Books, London)

Innes, W. T. *Exotic Aquarium Fishes* (Bailey Bros., London)

Kalliman, Dr Klaus *Enjoy Your Platys and Swordtails* (Pet Library, London)

Kelly, J. *Aquarists' Guide* (Pet Library, London)

La Carte, Rosario S. *Enjoy the Tetras* (Pet Library, London)

BIBLIOGRAPHY

McInerny, D. *Tropical Fish* (Foyle, London)

Schneider, E. (Ed) *Enjoy Your Tropical Fish Picture Book* (Pet Library, London)

Schneider, E. and Whitney, L. F. *Complete Guide to Tropical Fishes* (Nelson, London)

Schubert, Gottfried *Diseases of Aquarium Fishes* (Studio Vista, London)

Sonderberg, P. M. *Topical Fish and Aquaria* (Cassell, London)

Sterba, Gunther *Freshwater Fishes of the World* (Studio Vista, London)

Vorderwinkler, William *Breeding Egg-layers* (T.F.H. Publications, London)

Wachtell, Hellmuth *Aquarium Hygiene* (Studio Vista, London)

Weigel, Wilfried *Planning and Decorating the Aquarium* (Studio Vista, London)

Wickler, Wolfgang *Breeding Aquarium Fishes* (Studio Vista, London)

PERIODICALS

The following periodicals will be of interest to all owners of tropical fish.

Aquarist and Pondkeeper (The Butts, Half Acre, Brentford, Middlesex)

Petfish Monthly (554 Garratt Lane, London, S.W.17)

Tropical Fish Hobbyist (an American publication, obtainable through agents advertising in the British hobby publications)

Index

Trouble caused by incorrect
    feeding, 61
Tube, siphon, 5, 6
—, —, use of, 70
Tubifex worms, 49, 63
Two-spot barb, 52, Pl. 5

Undergravel filter, 7
Underwater plants, anchoring of,
    5, 12

Vacuum flask for transporting
    fish, 58
Vallisneria, 20, 21
— *spiralis*, 20
— *torta*, 21
Velvet spot, 91

Water, acid content of, 23
—, alkaline content of, 23
— fern, 16
—, filling tank with, 23
— flea, 63
—, hard, 23
—, milky, 73

— snails, 26
—, soft, 23
— sprite, 16
—, temperature of, 25
Wattage, tank heaters, 4
White cloud mountain minnow,
    30, 53, Pl. 9
White cloud mountain minnow,
    breeding, 82
White spot, 91
Widow, black, 31
Worm feeder, 8
—, shredder, 9, 66
—, tubifex, 49, 63
—, tubifex, breeding of, 64
—, white, 65
—, white, breeding of, 65
Wounds in fish, treatment of, 89

X-ray fish, 53, Pl. 8

Young and mature fish, relative
    merits, 59

Zebra fish, 53, Pl. 4